monsoonbooks

RED-LIGHT NIGHTS, BA

Sex journalist William Sparrow grew up in Chicago and _____ in a variety of industries before relocating to Asia in 2002. He became the Editor in Chief of one of Asia's leading sexuality websites, *Asian Sex Gazette* (www.asiansexgazette.com), and began reporting on issues of sexuality from cities across Asia. Willliam has a regular column, "Sex in Depth", in *Asia Times Online* (www.atimes.com). He currently lives in Thailand with his wife and daughter.

Red-light Nights, Bangkok Daze is his first book.

Red-light Nights, Bangkok Daze

William Sparrow

monsoon

monsoonbooks

Published in 2008
by Monsoon Books Pte Ltd
52 Telok Blangah Road
#03-05 Telok Blangah House
Singapore 098829
www.monsoonbooks.com.sg

ISBN: 978-981-08-1076-4
Copyright © William Sparrow, 2008

The moral right of the author has been asserted.

National Library Board Singapore Cataloguing in Publication Data
Sparrow, William, 1975-
Red-light nights, Bangkok daze / William Sparrow. – Singapore : Monsoon Books, 2008.
p. cm.
ISBN-13 : 978-981-08-1076-4 (pbk.)

1. Sex-oriented businesses – Asia. 2. Prostitution – Asia.
3. Prostitutes – Asia. I. Title.

HQ231.85
306.74095 -- dc22   OCN244366449

Printed in Singapore

12 11 10 09 08   1 2 3 4 5 6 7 8 9

Contents

FOREWORD 11

Red-light nights, Bangkok daze 15

Church has the last word in the Philippines 34

The anatomy of a Thai porn scandal 39

Indecent exposure in Indonesia 50

Thai go-go dancer becomes a porn star 55

The Philippines exports labor and sex 60

Getting your fill in the Philippines 64

Songkran: hard holiday for ladyboys 82

Indonesian model Tiara Lestar shakes things up 87

China Barbie takes on Mattel 92

The lady works alone—or does she? 97

Japan's Lolita merchants feel the heat 107

My big fat triad wedding 111

When freaky-deaky equals hara-kiri 125

Thailand's twin threat 129

When kissing cousins aren't so cute 135

Squeaky clean in Thailand 139

My short time with Tito 143

Thailand produces the world's smallest porn star   150

Asia's dangerous emperor syndrome   155

Cell swingers in Cambodia   160

The young ones   165

Bedding burlesque babes in Burma   172

A view on Vietnamese sex scandals   178

Go ugly early   183

By the numbers: consensual sex in Asia   187

The land of the Karma Sutra flunks sex ed   194

Grrl power Asia: hear it growl   199

Sex in the Chinese city   205

In Pakistan, a dark trade comes to light   211

AFTERWORD   217

ACKNOWLEDGEMENTS   223

Foreword

Welcome to William's world
By Simon Tearack

According to the world's oldest cliché, prostitution is the world's oldest profession. The claim is unverifiable, but whatever the truth, it seems likely that mere hours after an unnamed cave woman hit on the idea of exchanging sex for an extra chunk of mastodon steak, an enormous peripheral industry arose consisting pimps, *mamasan*s, and publicists. Moments after that an even larger industry of tribal and religious leaders, living off the avails of suppressing the sex industry and harassing its purveyors and their clientele, emerged.

Mastodons are now extinct; everyone else in the above paragraph is still doing a roaring trade. And nowhere are there more prostitutes, pimps, bargirls, *mamasan*s, erotic dancers, and erotic masseurs and masseuses than in Asia; and nowhere is the array of anti-sex crusaders, opportunistically moralistic politicians, hand-wringing clerics, and contradictory and hypocritical sex laws more bewildering.

For the past few years, the multicolored canvas of sex and sexuality in Asia has been portrayed in all its aspects—the good, the bad and the ugly—by William Sparrow on his website AsianSexGazette.com. Asian sex sites abound, of course, but ASG shunned pornography and blazed a new trail: "sex journalism", a rare attempt at honest, agenda-free coverage and analysis of actual news events linked to the sex trade and sex practices in general, on the world's largest, most populous and most diverse continent.

ASG's rapid increase in popularity was quite understandable. Asia, especially East and Southeast Asia, had long been known to Westerners as a sexual playground, with its vast platoons of friendly, extremely attractive women falling over one another to please male (and female, if the price was right) sex tourists. Yet mainstream media only reported the negative, sensational stories—about horrors such as under-age prostitution, human trafficking, disease, and sex slavery—to a degree that any objective traveler knew was misleading at best and sheer malicious fantasy at worst. Yes, those vices exist, but the bulk of the sex trade in Asia is nothing more than the business of pleasure, with well-paid sellers and satisfied customers. On ASG, writers had no need to fear reporting this simple truth, and those whose sensibilities, religion, morality or sheer hypocrisy made the truth unpalatable had no need to log on.

William Sparrow himself, like several of the site's contributors, has no bones about admitting his own indulgences in the sexual smorgasbords of Thailand, the Philippines, Hong Kong, China, and elsewhere. They, like many visitors to and expatriates in Asia, believe that recreational sex is a commodity to be bought and sold like any other human indulgence as long as it does no harm to the seller, or the buyer. And vicarious pleasures are indeed to be found on ASG by the envious Internet voyeur.

However, ASG shuns nothing but censorship itself, and its readers will find intermixed with stories of the brothels in Shenzhen, Singapore, Tokyo, Phnom Penh, and Mumbai, the lesbian shows in Bangkok's Soi Cowboy, the titillations of Makati's P Burgos Street, the high-rolling hookers of Wan Chai, Macau, and Singapore, and the gentle yet courageous sensuality of the horny Muslim women of Malaysia and Indonesia, the darker tales of sordid exploitation, of poverty, sexually transmitted disease, lack of sex education, and of the malfeasance and incompetence of governments and their accomplices in organized religion.

This book excerpts the writings of William Sparrow himself, and so in a sense only gives a taste of the panorama to be found on his websites (ASG has recently launched affiliate sites concentrating on other regions of the world), or on the general Asian news-analysis site Asia Times Online which, at the time of writing, runs a regular column by Sparrow. But it is bittersweet, not for the timid of palate.

As a self-styled sex journalist, Sparrow tells all. This is not about personal conquests; human frailty is as much a part of sexual adventurism as prowess is. Nor does he fall into the all-too-common trap of worshiping the women (Sparrow is proudly heterosexual) of the sex trade, though many sexually oppressed Western men fleeing the "liberated" but frigid, overindulged and often overweight creatures who dominate the "other half" back home understandably mistake Asia's nubile little sex machines for goddesses. No, divine though they seem, they are human too, often falling prey to greed, or malice, or just plain stupidity ("But you said you would marry me if I sucked it!").

The aim of journalism is above all to inform, hopefully to educate, certainly to entertain. This book, it is hoped, does all of the above.

Simon Tearack is the nom de plume of a Western journalist now living in Thailand who has edited and contributed articles to Asian Sex Gazette.

Red-light nights, Bangkok daze

Spending an evening in the tawdry red-light districts of Bangkok with old friends and new ones, some may begin to ponder the decadence and depravity on offer and the people who participate in one of Asia's most renowned sex tourist destinations.

Promised a tour and a night out with the guys, we planned to meet in Patpong, the central red-light district possibly as well known for its fake designer merchandise as its very real sex shows, go-go bars, and beer bars, all teeming with girls seemingly eager for male companionship.

Pondering the possible value for this article and other "research" I was doing, I considered for a moment checking out one of the sex shows I had so far avoided since first going to Bangkok years before. The fleeting experience I had had was, in essence, walking into one such establishment, getting a momentary look at the talent on stage and then fleeing; to me there are just some things you don't want to see being done with fruit or Ping-Pong balls. Not to mention that I feel there is nothing sexy about the female vagina being used as a bottle opener.

Shuddering at the thought of that experience, I chose instead to visit a pub-style bar on Patpong Soi 2. Unlike the many beer bars on the *soi* that are of the open-air variety, this bar is set low, with few windows, and even at the height of day the bar remains dimly lit.

A homey bar where the music is rarely raised to more than a dull background din, it has long been enjoyed by those looking for a refuge away from the blaring discos and go-go bars of Patpong. Some use this location as a place to relax after an exciting night out on the *soi*; I was there to warm up slowly for the night ahead.

When I entered the small bar, a boisterous coo sounded from the girls, most of whom knew me, and they jumped from their seats to greet me. Momentarily, I was concerned for an older gentleman at the end of the bar who seemed to have had his pacemaker reset by the sudden and unexpected excitement.

The few patrons in the bar took a moment to study the newcomer suspiciously, but they decided quickly that there was little reason for excitement and went back to nursing their drinks. The bar's *mamasan* smiled and *wai*ed me (the *wai* is a Thai greeting of respect, made by pressing one's palms together in a prayer-like motion). I returned the gesture and then quickly found the elder *mamasan*, who had piled herself into a dark corner of the bar; she is unmoved by much and my arrival thus far seemed unnoticed. I *wai*ed her and smiled; she gave an almost imperceptible nod and the faintest smile seemed to cross her face. Elders and those held in high esteem or respected are not expected to return the *wai*, but I had now officially arrived.

The girls say Patpong is quiet these days. They would never refer to their bar specifically—they expect it to be quiet—but Patpong has seen better days. "Not so many customers lately and police make problem [at the] bars too much," one of the girls who had worked this bar for years told me.

Interesting, because this very bar, for what it lacks in pretty girls, fresh faces and a happening crowd, has always enjoyed a certain favor, it seems, in the eyes of the law. When all the other bars have shuttered for the evening, this little pub crawls into the wee hours of the morning undisturbed by police so long as the customers want to stay.

The inevitable questions about my wife, who is Thai but was notably not with me that evening, came quick and fast. I assured them she was well and sent her regards. One of the "girls", who probably passed her prime at some point during the Vietnam War, tried in her sexiest voice and broken English to point out to me: "You in Patpong and go out alone tonight, I very lucky!" She groped me improperly just as I choked on a swig of beer.

"Not tonight, dear," I said to her with a smile. She pouted, something not easy for a fifty-year-old, but she did her best to pull it off.

The girls here are friends and have helped at times when I have needed it and I have tried to return the favor when I can. I have become an adoptee to this strange, dysfunctional family and it is a relationship that I hold in high regard.

Over the bar there is a wall covered in photos of babies and toddlers. I noted that there were a few more since the last time I was there. I took a moment to count the photos, or rather the babies in the pictures, and came to a total of about seventy-three. These are the "bar's babies", the *mamasan* will tell you proudly— babies had by girls who have worked at the bar and since gone off to greener pastures, usually in the form of marriage to a customer of foreign origin, a *farang*.

She has been collecting the photos and adding them to the wall for more than twenty years, far longer than many bars in this red-light district last.

"You have baby, you give me picture, okay?" she said; it was more of a directive than a request.

Smiling, I confirmed that I would, though I did take a moment to consider that my wife has never worked here. I think. Anyway, this is not a woman to split hairs with.

I thanked them for everything and soon after draining my

beer, promised to visit again.

Finding myself again roaming the streets, I decided on a livelier go-go bar and figured that with sixty or so girls and thirty or forty customers, I could blend in and enjoy some anonymity. This assumption would prove incorrect.

Heading for the back of the bar while being groped by innumerable women, I finally located a seat, ordered a drink, and got comfortable. On the sizable stage before me twenty or so gorgeous—and some not so gorgeous—girls wriggled away to booming Western pop tunes dressed in tiny bikinis. I found that I might have chosen my seat poorly; this corner spot at the back had put me far too close to the DJ and his formidable sound system. The base shook my seat and rattled the very soul. But I tried to relax anyway, enjoy my beer and take in the "ambiance".

A journalist needs contacts, and innumerable stories have been built on the leads, tips, and sources from people whom I regard as friends who have given me information over the years here. Yet a red-light district is also a place where a man wants to enjoy a measure of anonymity.

I didn't notice the familiar photographer making his way through the bar until he was nearly in front of me. This man makes his livelihood plying the streets of Patpong taking "holiday snaps" of tourists and selling them. Obviously these are not your average Disney-type family holiday photos. Many are lurid, sexy keepsakes that I imagine many of the men hide—if they keep them at all.

I was probably distracted by the girl on stage who kept smiling at me flirtatiously—she was an unusual example of a bargirl in that she had designer glasses and braces. Firstly, the expense of braces and glasses is often forgone by bar girls, who are there because of their financial woes to begin with; and secondly, it gave her a young "schoolgirl" look. I decided immediately that she probably does well, very well.

Abruptly, I became aware of the photographer, who seemed just as surprised to happen upon me in the crowd. He stopped short for a second and gave me a respectful *wai*, to which I nodded and gave a smile. He waved, gave a quick smile, and continued wading through the crowd, hoping to make a few bucks.

As quickly as it had happened I realized its effect. Although a few of the *farang* customers in the crowd seemed to notice, the action was not lost on the numerous bar girls dancing on stage, or the nearby *mamasan* keeping a watchful eye on all that was happening in her club. The set soon ended and the girls on stage began to exit, only to be dutifully replaced by another two dozen girls dressed in bras and G-string panties. For many of those exiting the stage, I found that I was a target of opportunity and interest.

Four or five girls descended, cooing, groping, complimenting, and questioning me: "Handsome man!" "What your name?" "Big man!" "Where you come from?" "You buy drink for me?" "What you do Thailand?" The *mamasan* was poised nearby, I assume just in case I decided to yell, "Champagne for everyone!" She could probably issue the drink tab faster than a trader on the floor of the New York Stock Exchange.

At about the same point I became aware of the number of customers who were eyeing me inappreciatively and suspiciously. I thought I overheard a Brit nearby say, "What's up with this fucking punter?"

The girls needed to be dispersed, and quickly. To my delight the "schoolgirl" was among the girls who were now attempting to suffocate me with their breasts. Grabbing her, I asked her name and offered to buy her a drink—all while speaking in Thai.

She seemed a bit shocked at my ability to speak her language, but played the part of being sheepishly flattered. It also effectively dispersed the crowd. I had chosen my companion and they knew that this *farang* was not going to be buying a half-dozen lady drinks—this one was not a greenhorn.

"*Farang chalat mak*! (This foreigner knows too much!)" one of the girls scoffed playfully as she walked off.

Left alone with the schoolgirl, I was able to grab the opportunity to probe a little deeper with an impromptu interview. After some initial niceties and her taking the requisite six seconds to drain a tiny US$3 Coke and request another, which I provided, she finally started to answer some basic questions.

"I am from Bangkok," she said rather assertively, which in itself was also a rarity. Most of the girls working the bars are from farms outside the city, from the farmlands of the Northeast known as Isaan, and are seeking an escape from rural poverty. But it was plausible; from all initial indicators she was more refined and worldly than most other bargirls and her complexion was nearly white—something the tanned farm girls hold in high regard as a beauty and status symbol.

To queries about family she was less forthcoming, but I soon stumbled on to a subject that she was keen to speak about: education. She claimed to be a student in one of the local universities, where she studied travel, wanting to become a stewardess, or at least work for an airline.

"If not, maybe I can become a travel agent. I want to travel!" Her story seemed to be panning out, her English was among the most flawless examples I had encountered in a long time, and at her age had to be a product of good education. If not, she had this role-play thing down cold, and was milking the schoolgirl angle for all it was worth.

"My parents took me to Malaysia when I was younger—it is very beautiful. We also have gone to Cambodia. I did not like it too much. Cambodia is very poor," she told me authoritatively, as if I might not have heard. Many Thais struggle against poverty so international travel, even to neighboring countries, is unheard of, so once again her story seemed solid.

"So why are you working in a bar? Is it to pay for school?" I asked.

Apparently such a notion—that a bargirl could make enough funds to pay for a university education—was absurd, and just the look on her face told me this.

"No, my parents pay for school. But they cannot pay for much more. I work here to take care of myself and buy things I want. I bought these glasses and had my teeth set," she said, fingering her glasses and smiling broadly. "What do you think? Good?"

I conceded that they were nice. She began listing things she was thinking about getting; among them was the popular nose job to "fix" her flat Thai nose and make it more beautiful like a Westerner's nose with a more pronounced bridge.

Suddenly some kind of unheard "two-minute warning" sounded and she realized she had to go dance again. At about the same time, she also noticed she had barely touched her second lady drink—all this talking had led her to neglect her duty of draining as many of these as possible on a customer's tab (for which she would receive a commission).

Seeing this coming, I pressed a couple of folded THB100 notes into her hands. She smiled a metallic beam of joy, hugged me roughly, and then began bouncing a few times in a manner that is hard to explain before playfully kissing my cheek and taking to the stage.

It was a good time to make an escape. I settled with the *mamasan*, who was disapproving that I had failed to barfine one of her girls. She looked me over with a final look of suspicion and walked off in a huff.

Something tamer was in order, and the guys would be

meeting up with me shortly. I settled on a beer bar, which is a standard open-air-style bar popular throughout Thailand. The girls there are generally fully clothed, the prices are lower, and the girls are usually not overly friendly in such an open environment. It also offered the advantage of allowing me to watch out for my wayward mates as they made their way through the carnal humanity of Patpong.

I might have chosen poorly again—I have a marriage to keep together, mind you. A seat was had and a beer obtained. Since it was still relatively early, the bar had few girls. Most of them hovered around me, testing my Thai, cooling me off with a little moist towel. Massaging, planting an occasional kiss and, as always, groping. With girls in places like this I use Thai immediately and it generally impresses them. It also, as planned, led to the inevitable loaded question: "How did you learn Thai?"

"*Mee mia khon Thai laeo* (I have a Thai wife already)," I said, flashing the wedding band as evidence

There was some initial disappointment, but it was fleeting. The girls regrouped and tried a secondary approach.

"*Mai bpen rai, chan bpen mia noi khun kuen nee* (Don't worry about it, I will be your 'small wife' tonight)," one of the notably cutest and sexiest girls proclaimed.

A weary growl escaped me—she was very cute. I bought her and her friend each a lady drink and for a few moments it stopped her from propositioning me.

Taking a *mia noi* is a practice in Thailand whereby a man takes a lover or mistress, usually much younger than his wife. It is reserved for middle- and upper-class Thai men, as the man must be able to provide financial support both for his primary family and his mistress (and each one after that). Polygamy is illegal in Thailand but still not uncommon in the upwardly mobile classes of the country. In earlier days it was not unusual for a middle/

upper-class man to take a wife of equal standing, then choose a *mia noi* of his liking, only to be augmented by a "slave girl" that he could "purchase" from a destitute family to work as a maid. Nevertheless, the maid could be called upon to produce children, not to mention sexual gratification of her beau as he desired.

This phenomenon gained some attention years back when some government ministers calling for greater transparency of their membership asked that personal finances be disclosed. There was an outcry among the ministers, but not because they feared it would expose graft; rather that it would make taking and keeping a *mia noi* impossible. In what later would become a soundbite of this controversy, one minister declared, "It is a man's right to have a *mia noi*!"

While it may be a right among Thai men, it certainly does not apply to *farang*. Thai women seem to have figured out that in our Western culture, such a practice is taboo and thus forbid their *farang* husbands from having a *mia noi*.

The bargirls obviously know this, but it does not stop them suggesting the arrangement. But as a *farang* married to a Thai, taking a *mia noi* would be at my peril.

While I was considering the implications of having a *mia noi*, my mates showed up. Thank god.

As my friends started to arrive, I could pretend not to be taken by the cutie who continued to massage my thigh and occasionally kiss my cheek. As each of my mates arrived, they were greeted and attended to in the same affectionate manner.

I was told that Soi Cowboy is much more of a happening scene these days than Patpong or, in their opinion, Nana Plaza. So a plan was forged to relocate our motley gang to Soi Cowboy for more entertainment.

A brief taxi ride and we spilled out on to the glittering street of Soi Cowboy and went first to a bar that seemed to cater to a

Japanese fetish. The girls at this venue dress in uniforms similar to Japanese schoolgirls, but the key here is that one article of clothing is missing: the panties.

Girls dance sexily on the mirrored ground-floor stage and on a second floor, which has a glass floor. Patrons—mostly Japanese—sit below and crane their necks at the girls dancing above, getting a sexy, though fleeting glimpse of the girls' nether regions.

It is a recipe that has spelled success among Japanese tourists and the bar was packed. Finding a seat was nearly impossible and made the view less interesting. We moved on to another bar.

The next bar was more the typical go-go-style venue, with the girls dancing naked on a central stage. There were bar stools situated around the stage and booths set back from it—all of which seemed to be occupied. We decided the up-close-and-personal seats stage side would suffice.

Beers and whiskeys were ordered as the girls jiggled, shimmied, and danced seductively and occasionally flirted with us.

Soon the lights came up slightly, the music changed from booming pop tunes to a slow and more erotic R&B blend, and the girls on stage made their exit. I assumed it was just another rotation of the girls on stage, but I was wrong.

The lights were again dimmed and stage lights above from the second floor alerted us to a half-dozen naked women, four of whom were snaking their way down the poles set around the stage. Once on stage they began a seductive dance among themselves, with the girls paired off in two couples. It was a lesbian show.

The couple immediately in front of us was stunning. One of the girls was the all-natural Thai girl, small breasts, thin, long legs, and raven hair. Her partner was no less stunning, though less natural, as she had had a breast augmentation that, while not excessive, gave her a more curvaceous figure than most Thai women's. She, of course, had the same long legs, dark-brown hair, and brown eyes.

The girls swayed sexily and rhythmically to the music, concentrating more on one another than anyone around them. They kissed tenderly, running their hands through one another's long, black, silken hair. Soon each of them was licking, sucking, and biting her way along her "lover's" body, breasts, and thighs. Playfully they feigned this foreplay a bit longer before dropping to the floor in a mutual embrace. They took turns performing oral sex on one another in myriad positions. These girls were not faking these acts: our stage-side seats offered confirmation that they were in fact performing oral sex on one another.

I admit I was transfixed by this performance, and finally one of the girls noticed me staring at her slack-jawed. She giggled and whispered something to her partner, then demanded: "Ice?!" She held out her hand to me and I realized that I was sitting with my drink poised halfway to my mouth, where it had stalled. I downed the whiskey in a single gulp and slammed the glass on the stage; she smiled coyly and scooped a handful of ice from the glass, took a mouthful and rubbed the rest over her lover's body while sucking on her breasts.

This exhibition of lust culminated in all four girls—two of whom I had barely noticed up to this point—coming together as four writhing bodies of lesbian loving. In all my years in Bangkok I had never seen a show performed quite so lustfully.

The lights came up and the music changed sets. I commented to my friends that we had chosen our seats wisely in this instance. The beauty with the augmented cleavage blew me a kiss as she exited the stage, toweling herself off. A new troupe of dancing girls took the stage. I needed a drink.

Meanwhile one of my friends was deep in conversation with a bargirl who clearly understood less than 1% of what he was saying, but she smiled affectionately and said, "Yes, *chai*, *chai*," at key moments. Another was trying to figure out what a bargirl thinks of South Asian men. The verdict: positive, if he can pay.

Another one of my friends who had joined me announced that he was leaving. We protested as best we could and even the random bargirl attempted to tackle him back into his seat, but he was off for the evening. A good time had by all, but he too had a wife at home and would be a good boy on this evening.

I assisted one of the remaining mates by speaking for moment in Thai to his chosen partner for the evening. I determined quickly that she was "just off the bus" and could speak little English. No matter, she liked my friend.

"*Khao naalak, khao phut Engrit faneg lao mai kao jai, choap*! (He's cute, talks a lot in English I don't understand, but I like him!)" she said.

I was happy to see one of the girls from the lesbian show approaching me. Was I beckoning her, or was she circling her prey?

I bought her drinks as we all began considering a move to an "after hours" nightspot, as it was getting late and the go-go bars would be closing soon. My augmented angel, whom I now knew as Ao, was keen to come along, so I struck a tentative deal with her and paid her barfine. My friends did the same and we now had companionship for the evening.

The girls slipped away for a few moments to change from their G-strings in to some street clothes. When they returned I considered for a moment that Ao's outfit was still hardly appropriate—heels, an ultra-short miniskirt that did not hide the fact that she was wearing a G-string, and a shirt that was seemingly more of a corset, but it did accentuate her cleavage nicely.

We moved to a bar off Soi Cowboy that stays open until the wee hours of the morning. We concentrated on beer and the girls turned their attention to food.

Settling in, I chatted with Ao. She seemed content with her free food and drink, and the THB1,000 (US$25) arrangement I offered for her company and conversation. She spoke openly and seemed to prefer English to deciphering my basic Thai—fine with me.

What unfolded was a somewhat standard tale one often hears from these girls. She was from the Northeast region known as Isaan, her family are poor rice farmers and she came to Bangkok to work and help herself and her family. Thais are very communal in caring for their family. It is not unusual for a girl who plies her trade in these bars to send most of what she earns back to the family to support them, and even an extended family that may consist of children born to their siblings, but whom the siblings cannot support.

She claimed to be twenty-two years old and had worked the bars for three years. She said she liked it, but I pressed her on this several times. Conceding that the work was tiring and emotionally stressful, she agreed that it was not easy, but that she would rather be doing this—for the money she earns—than staying at home and working in the rice fields. Besides, she said with a devilish grin, "It is a lot more fun."

Speaking of fun, it was time to get to an issue that, for me anyway, was quite intriguing: the lesbian show. I asked her if she liked doing the show.

"It is okay, we make more money, the girls who make [show]," she said. "And customers like [it, so] I get better customer, and can ask man pay more." The devilish smile returned. "Did you like the show?" she asked flirtatiously.

"Yes, yes I did," I admitted. What she had just said about her rates and customers begged another question, though; I asked if she was often bar-fined with her partner and asked to go with customers for a threesome.

"Yes, we do that a lot too!" she said, rolling her eyes and laughing. Luckily her laughter and the bar's music drowned out the reflexive whimper that escaped me as I conjured up a mental image. I found that she was looking at me coyly again—time to get back on track.

The show was so real and the girls so taken with one another that the next set of questions was automatic: Did she like women, or at least her partner in the show?

Her partner turned out to be a very good friend who had been at the bar almost as long as she had, and it was where they had become close friends. Apparently, the *mamasans* had chosen the prettiest girls and those who had naturally paired up through friendship for the possibility of working the lesbian show. I surmised this was to avoid rivalry and to build upon existing relationships.

"She is very good friend, but we [are] just friends!" she scolded me. "I like man!"

I decided to take a different angle. I asked her about Thai men. She said she was indifferent to them, but pointed out that they could not take very good care of her (by her standards, of course). I had stumbled on to something here, because as the conversation flowed she offered, without being pressed, that she had lost her virginity to a Thai man when she was fifteen. It turned out he was not very good to her and was soon having sex with someone else. As I pried more and more, I found that the experiences she had had with Thai men had been mediocre at best.

Switching back to women, I asked about her relationship with sisters, female friends, and girls at the bar. The last query bore fruit.

"There was girl who worked [in the] same bar as me. I went with customer one night. I like him very much. He good man and very nice to me," she said with scorn that only because I have a Thai wife alerted me to what was coming. "He come back bar one night and I go with customer already. This 'lady' take customer me!" she said on the edge of a pouting rage.

I knew better than to launch into a line of questions about the fact that she was in fact with a customer already—loyalty is for the man, not the working girl.

"What happened to the girl?" I asked. It turned out to be the right question.

"I don't know," she said, seemingly dropping the topic with a devious glint in her eye. "She not work bar same me anymore." She said this with the type of satisfaction that can only be described as a sort of alpha-female standing among the girls of the bar.

Alpha-females, as I have come to call them, in the bar trade are the most beautiful, command the highest prices and generally fall into a clique consisting mostly of other "alphas", or occasionally a young newcomer they see as having potential. The quieter, plainer girls work to steer clear of drawing their angst, as being on their bad side can make the workplace unbearable for the non-alpha. *Mamasan*s will even cave in to alpha-girls' demands, occasional unannounced days off, and prima donna attitudes as they are big earners and attract customers.

Another girl taking an alpha-girl's previous customer is seemingly a capital offense in this world and behind-the-scenes catfights can be common.

The conversation came full circle to her partner: "So your partner would never go with your customer?"

"Partner" confused her for a second and I was rewarded with a name after an explanation. "No, Jin would never go with a man I go with already, and I not take customer her," she said as a matter of law. So, I couldn't take Jin, I thought; but when presenting this question, Ao decided I could, if I took both of them and Jin wanted to go.

Probing her relationship with Jin further, I asked about their friendship, and was regaled with tales far too tame to relate here. But when something resembling the endearing emotion of love appeared in her eyes, I again probed their physical relationship. Asking how it felt for her to perform those very sexual acts with her friend, I moved tentatively toward the truth I sought.

"She is good friend, and yes it is same sex. But not same because show, and we do many times. Sometimes it feels good, but it is mostly just trying to do the show and have fun." She shrugged it off.

"What about when you go with a customer together? Then you are with a man and I am sure you guys continue your 'act'. How does it feel sexually for you then?" I asked.

"Sex with man I like, I tell you already," she said, thinking that I might be drunk, or just not so clever. "When we go together with customer, same working, is more good two lady go with customer—man finish very quickly!" She giggled again.

Good, she was having fun again. Tempting perilously thin ice, I pried again, asking if she had ever had a sexual experience with Jin that was not with a customer, just themselves. She looked momentarily skittish. Maybe I had gone too far—she took much longer than usual to speak up again.

"One time we go with customer, he very handsome and funny, we like very much. He [was a] young man, but he drink too much!" She was pouting again. "He take off everything [and he] shower with us and go bed. We come out *horng nam, khao bpai norn laeo*!" (When they came out of the bathroom, he was asleep already.)

It was good that she was beginning to open up and had suddenly switched from broken English to Thai with me—she was talking to me on the level. It was easy to find out what happened next. "*Tom arai*? (So what did you do?)" I asked playfully.

They tried everything to wake him up, short of setting him on fire. Apparently he had paid them a lot; they liked him and wanted to make sure that he felt he'd got his money's worth. Jin performed oral sex on him while Ao kissed him, playfully slapped him, and slithered up his abdomen, grinding her genitalia across his torso.

"DRINK PLEASE!" I called out abruptly and reflexively.

All of this was to no avail apparently, as this poor bastard slumbered on and the girls sat back frustrated. Frustration that was mixed with lust. (For readability, Ao's account follows in English.)

"I don't know what happened, but I found myself in an embrace joking with Jin about the guy and wishing he was awake. She asked me if I was horny and I admitted I was. Jin did not say anything but kissed me and smiled. Then she started kissing my breasts too; at first I was startled, but I did not stop her—it felt good!

"Soon she was eating my pussy and it was too much, she does it in the show and I have had men do it and I cannot come, but it was only a minute or so and I came. I just lay there stunned for a few minutes and Jin held me. I felt really good.

"Jin knows I do not like to perform cunnilingus so much, so I tried to help her masturbate, but she stopped me and told me it was okay, that she just wanted me to feel good."

I found I was having a hard time not falling out of the chair at this point. She once again noticed my slack-jaw expression and showed a moment of trepidation for having said too much. I reassured her it was okay and she was her giggly self again within seconds.

Not for a moment, even a second, of this evening had the fact been lost on me that I was sitting with possibly the sexiest, personally demure, and overtly sexual woman I had ever met in my life. As the evening developed and she pecked me on my cheek, or dropped an affirmative hand on my leg, I was aware of the one hundred or so Western men who looked on, occasionally with jealousy—and possibly with hatred. As a Western man, I appreciated the company. This woman exuded sexuality, in every sense of the word.

Liquor flowed, stories were exchanged and friends renewed their bonds. This was not just a place for the tourist, or rather the sex tourist, but it was also a place where expats, and Thais themselves, gathered for an escape from the reality that is daily life. These girls offered that escape, through fantasy and the fantastic. The boundaries were indeed usually limitless and through a mix of money, monogamy, and maturity a limit was defined by the individuals themselves.

There was nothing wrong with these girls or the situation in which they found themselves. By and large—at a level I can say with a measure of experience—the girls were here voluntarily, knowing what was on offer and what was at stake when they entered the profession. Of the women I spoke to, I could only rarely find a one who was willing to have sex without a condom; sex education has been effective in Thailand. Asked about abuse, the women would not tolerate it; from the bar staff or from customers.

Am I advocating prostitution? Saying that sex work is the way beautiful young women of Thailand should unequivocally accept without question? Absolutely not. But I will say without spinning the numbers that this is a tourist and domestic industry that, with or without intervention, is going to continue to flourish.

Feminists may cry foul, anti-prostitution campaigners may decry what I say. I understand. Maybe, sometimes they have not actually met the girls spinning this trade and are simply pushing a moralistic, holier-than-thou viewpoint. They may not have had the chance to balance the negative with the positive outlets and effects it can have for many of these women. In some cases it could even be viewed as an opportunity for them in a society where few exist.

I was again reminded that I was the prey and this woman the hunter as she leaned into me and kissed me tenderly and romantically. My friends had gone and we walked slowly down the now-darkened street of Soi Cowboy. The evening was coming to a close. Ao asked again if I would take her with me, again pouting. I kissed her again and got into the taxi. In a whiskey-induced daze I decided that it had been yet another very good night in Bangkok.

Church has the last word in the Philippines

The Philippines' Department of Education (DepEd) is aggressively trying to push through a sex education plan for high-school students, despite protests and lobbying of the Catholic Church, which seeks to muzzle educators from presenting what it considers to be "immoral" information.

DepEd must clear a final hurdle from the Presidential Council on Values Formation (PCVF)—the body which is currently reviewing the secondary schools' "adolescent reproductive health manuals", according to Education Secretary Jesli A Lapus.

"The new draft modules, which are subject to PCVF review and approval, are purely health and science angles on reproductive health ... They are not sex educational materials at all," Lapus told the *Philippine Daily Inquirer* this week after DepEd furnished the newspaper with copies of the revised manual titled *Secondary Teachers' Toolkit on Adolescent Reproductive Health*.

Lapus stressed that the revised modules were "products of nationwide multisectoral consultations".

Although the Philippines has been given positive marks in recent decades for its sex education programs, in the past few years that progress has steadily eroded. Getting past PCVF is likely to be a formidable challenge as there is a strong presence of the Catholic clergy on the council, which is chaired by President Gloria Macapagal-Arroyo, who is also known for bending to pressure from the Church.

In 2005, Arroyo told the UN General Assembly to "respect the deep Catholicism of the Filipino people" and said that natural family planning is more effective than artificial means like condoms. Her statements prompted outrage from activists and non-governmental organizations.

The Church in the Philippines—where more than 85% of people are Catholic—has long held what many observers view as a negative influence on sexual and reproductive health. In an era of HIV/AIDS it seems staggering that a government, or even a church for that matter, would advocate what appears to be a "head in the sand approach" that puts citizens and parishioners at risk.

Statistics as of 2005 showed the country's annual population growth to be 2%, compared to India's 1.7% and Thailand's 1.3%. The study also found that there are over 470,000 illegal abortions performed in the Philippines each year, nearly 80,000 of which result in complications leading to hospitalization. Of course, abortion is illegal too in this Catholic society, leading to the practice of dangerous back-alley operations.

"The government's bending to the policies of the Church is a key force that is setting back reproductive and sexual health in the country," said Rhodora Roy-Raterta, executive director of the Family Planning Organization of the Philippines, at a 2005 conference. In the past she has called the Church a major hindrance to reproductive health and sex education.

"Public policy on family planning choice is also seen as a moral issue, which has drawn the Catholic hierarchy," she added.

The Catholic Church views condom use as promoting adultery and pre-marital sex, and church leaders believe that sex is meant solely for procreation between a husband and wife. In this context, using condoms—even for HIV/AIDS prevention—

becomes an immoral, sinful act. An "unnatural" act meant solely for pleasure.

The problem is becoming very real. An AIDS crisis threatens the Philippines as the number of people who are HIV positive has doubled in just over three years, the Health Department warned in 2006, echoing earlier concerns raised by the UN. A Health Department study at that time projected that the number of HIV carriers had risen to 11,168 from about 6,000 in 2002, Health Secretary Francisco Duque was quoted as saying to local media.

The Philippines, now home to around eighty-five million people, has become one of the fastest-growing populations in Asia with about two million new births each year, many of them in public hospitals so overwhelmed that new mothers are forced to share beds. Meanwhile, the country's population is projected to expand, based upon current trends, to as many as 142 million by 2040, according to the government's own estimates. The rapid arrival of new mouths to feed is already straining the country's creaking infrastructure and choking its efforts to cut poverty.

While family size has fallen to 3.5 children per woman—from six in the 1970s—Filipino mothers, on average, still have one more child than they intended to, according to research by the Alan Guttmacher Institute.

Three point five: consider that for a moment while Japan struggles with a birth rate of 1.1 per female; that the Japanese do not re-populate causes long-term economic and labor problems for the country. There, the conundrum is turned on its head. An industrialized nation and economic power like Japan needs children in a society structured around youngsters supporting the elderly through a "social security" system, like in the US. However, while Japan provides opportunities for its new generation, the soaring birth rate in the Philippines only seems to exacerbate poverty.

Beth Angsioco, chair of the Democratic Socialist Women of the

Philippines, said her group will join the campaign to press DepEd to continue reintegrating lessons on adolescent reproductive health into the secondary-school curriculum.

Angsioco said other groups, such as the Philippine Women Legislator's Committee on Population and Development and the Theia Initiative, will start their own signature-gathering drives to ensure that there will be no let-up in the campaign to have sex education taught in high schools.

"Teaching the youth the ABCs of reproductive health and responsible parenthood would help prevent 'accidents' such as teen pregnancies or, worse, sexually transmitted diseases. The youth should be empowered through knowledge," Angsioco said. "The Church should help, not hinder, young people from rising above the immorality of ignorance."

Sunny Cortes, leader of Aksyon LGBT (Lesbians, Gays, Bisexuals, and Transsexuals), agreed saying, "There is no reason why DepEd should not push through with the module. Most of us youth are learning sex and sexuality from the wrong sources, like peers, classmates, and pornographic materials," he said.

The Inquirer reported this week that the revised modules include teaching notes on pre-marital sex, commercial sex, abortion, and homosexuality. High-risk sexual practices are also discussed and classes are urged to debate the long-term health and social consequences of sexual risk-taking. However, the new textbooks stress sexual abstinence among adolescents, and ask teachers to lead discussions on the advantages of delaying sexual activities during adolescence.

In the end, so much emphasis has been given to women's rights and sex in the Islamic world in recent years that sometimes it can be overlooked that religious fanaticism and conservatism in any form can have extensive negative effects on people's reproductive rights. The Catholic Church's centuries-old doctrine on sex only for procreation leaves many people ignorant about sexual health. This is the sad reality.

Taking away people's right to protect themselves, their right to education, and to responsibly manage their sex lives is certainly taking away some of their humanity.

First published April 5, 2008 in *Asia Times Online*

The anatomy of a Thai porn scandal

In a case not unlike the Miss Jammu Anara Gupta sex-video scandal in Kashmir, where a former beauty queen stands accused of appearing in a pornography video, the Natt Chanapa scandal in Thailand is proving to be an arduous saga for the young Thai starlet.

On August 2, 2004 the mainstream, although not yet well-known, twenty-three-year-old actress Natt Chanapa (a.k.a Kesarin Chaichalermpol, Natt Kesarin, or simply Nong Natt) was discovered by authorities to have appeared in a hardcore pornography video that was being distributed on the black market and the Internet.

Chanapa, who is accused of performing in the hardcore pornographic film, claims that since the accusation made media headlines, modeling and advertising companies, magazine executives, and television producers have been offering her six-digit sums for modeling work.

The actress made the revelation after she sought help from the Law Society of Thailand for legal support regarding the police accusation. It is against Thai law to perform in pornographic films.

The deputy commander of the registration division, Colonel Wisut Wanibutr, who had accused her of acting in a hardcore film with a Japanese man, said that he had only carried out his duty and had not forced the actress to turn herself in to police.

"Many people believe that what I did was wrong. That is up to them. I issued the summons. She has the right to come or not," Wisut said.

Wisut earlier transferred Chanapa's case to the Crime Suppression Division after the actress refused to meet him regarding the case.

Indeed, meeting with police may only add to her woes, as any questions she answers or statements she makes are likely to incriminate her more and possibly lead to her prosecution. When the case broke in mid-2004, the actress sought legal assistance from the Law Society of Thailand, which advised that an earlier statement to the press, in which she had said she was "not willing" to act in the movie, could be used against her and that she should remain silent on the issue.

Law Society of Thailand human-rights attorney Nakhon Chatichompu said Chanapa should not have given interviews to the media, because those statements could be used against her in court.

For instance, he said, the actress told a television host that she "was not willing to act" in the film. "In a legal interpretation, this might portray her as having some intent to act. If she had used the words 'I was forced' there would be less impact on her case," he said.

Colonel Pinit Maneerat, superintendent of Wang Thonglang Police Station, said the actress had filed libel charges against the weekly magazine *Variety Maya Channel*. Police summoned the magazine's owner, executive editor, and publisher to face charges related to the case.

"If they are found guilty, they will be liable to a jail term, but they may settle out of court," he said.

Unlike her American counterparts, such as Paris Hilton who

appeared on a grainy, night vision-style sex tape with her then boyfriend Rick Solomon, the Nong Natt tape is quasi-professional, even rising above amateur-level hardcore pornography.

Such hardcore pornography is technically illegal in Thailand and the actress could face a jail term or fine. However, the summons that was issued in July 2004 and that is being reiterated this week in August 2004 by Thailand's Crime Suppression Division simply asks that the actress appear to answer questions regarding the ongoing investigation. It does not compel or require her to appear, and thus far Chanapa has chosen not to meet with police.

Culture and politics

Thailand's Buddhist-majority culture is generally conservative about sexuality, in the typical Asian sense. This is in deep contrast to the notorious reputation that the country has gained for prostitution, live sex shows, sex tourism, and red-light districts.

Yet the government works constantly to keep these "dark influences" in check and to restrain, at least, the sex and pornography industries. The Thai government even employs a special section of its police force, consisting of computer experts, to constantly seek out Thai pornography on the Internet and block access to it within the country. In some cases, this unit even tracks down and prosecutes adult-content webmasters and producers when they are located in Thailand.

Yet for all the pomp and circumstance of the Chanapa case and Thailand's omnipresent war on dark influences, the people themselves seem less than concerned with the seemingly consensual video Natt has made and with pornography in general.

Chanapa became instantly popular based on the media and police attention she gained as a result of the investigation, and has been offered large sums for mainstream acting and modeling jobs.

In addition, and far more striking, is the widespread mainstream interest in the video itself. It would seem that if only ten copies of the illicit video compact disc (VCD) were in Thailand before the story broke, by the following day millions of copies were changing hands throughout the country.

But what's most fascinating about this development is that the heavy circulation of the video has not been limited to the back-alley pirate VCD shops of Patpong. Instead, the video has made its way into the homes and businesses of middle-class, and even upper-class Thailand. Hotel employees from major resorts say that the video was being sold among the staff for THB20 (US$0.50) each, and employees were snapping them up.

Indeed, while compiling this story, I encountered a group of female massage therapists from a high-end Hua Hin, Thailand resort and spa—a location visited by David and Victoria Beckham. These refined, skilled, and often well-educated women giggled and blushed when they admitted, "Yes, we bought it and watched it together in a private staff lounge."

"It was good!" exclaimed a female resort employee, who continued, "[Police] want to pretend that sex is not a part of our culture, or that it is somehow 'bad' and 'evil'. But the video shows a very real Thai woman, a star, having and enjoying sex. Considering that we live in a culture, a country where maybe hundreds of thousands of women work in prostitution, it seems silly to me."

It would seem that the government's effort to suppress the illicit material has only served to fan the flames of Chanapa's popularity and that of the video itself, taking the underground video from the shadowy black market and thrusting it into mainstream pop culture.

In an effort to research for this article, of course, I stopped the first video hawker I saw just off the notorious Patpong red-light district and asked for the Nong Natt video, to see for myself. The vendor immediately perked up at the fact that a non-Thai was asking for the video, breaking into a wide grin.

He didn't have it on him, naturally; instead a few whispers to a cohort and a runner was off in the frenetic foot traffic to fetch it. Minutes later, during which the hawker tried to sell me a myriad of other movies, fake Rolexes, and finally porn that he promised was of only Thai women, the runner returned with an unmarked, plainly packed VCD and asked for THB120 (US$3.50). I finally knocked him down to THB100 (US$3)—*farang* prices, you understand.

Watching the video with my wife and another couple was a strange experience, not at all erotic—and I had no desire for it to be. But they wanted to see it too; "Can't I lend it to you tomorrow?" I asked.

This video was the real thing. This was no production with a shaky camera, dim lights, night vision, or otherwise absurd or questionable celebrity pornography. The pictures were clear, the shots were steady and the lighting was good. Not to mention that multiple cameras were employed, vibrators were used, oral sex was performed (by the Japanese actor, of course), and sex was had. It was quite typical of the fashion one finds in Japanese porn (except without the fuzzy bits over the furry bits). If Nong Natt had refused to participate, it must have been off camera.

But this by a mainstream Thai actress? Unthinkable!

Nevertheless, as damning as this may seem to the conservative watchdogs within Thailand's law-enforcement circles, the general acceptance of such material and Chanapa's mainstream following—as evidenced by the popularity of the video amongst the general public and by the "legitimate" entertainment industry's embrace of Chanapa after the story broke—seem to indicate that, no matter the level of pressure and prosecution that the government levies at Chanapa, it will only serve to bolster her popularity, while undermining the prosecution's and the court's ability to enforce any type of sentence due to negative public opinion regarding any punishment of Chanapa.

Unlike the sex-video scandal involving Anara Gupta and the ongoing court battle being waged in India, there has not been a public outcry in Thailand for pornography law reforms or pressure to prosecute by the public. This makes it unlikely that the Chanapa case will ever be fully prosecuted or, even if it is, that any subsequent penalties would be excessively harsh or worth the prosecution's efforts.

At least for the time being, Thais in general seem to be taking their characteristic *mai bpen rai* (don't worry about it) approach to this issue—an approach that authorities may also be considering.

December 2004, Act II

It seems that while investigating the Nong Natt pornography scandal, the police apparently failed to stop by their local black-market video hawker and ask him if he had any other videos relevant to the case.

This must be so because already making the rounds is a second video, as yet unmentioned by the police and generally unknown to most of the Thai public. This additional title appears to be a compilation of scenes that Chanapa did at different times during her "pornography career".

The video is broken down into three scenes: one is a sexy little dance and striptease, the next is a masturbation scene (with and without sexual aids), and the last one is another full-on sex scene with a Japanese actor—if not same actor from the first video then at least a different scene. If, as she claims about her first video, she was "not willing" to act in this video, then she must be a good actress indeed, as she looks quite happy, enjoying herself immensely.

So it would seem that this video will help the prosecution to prove that the first video was more than just a one-off production, and it undermines her "not willing" stance on her participation. Indeed, given that the video appears to have been shot at multiple locations (hotels), it would seem that Nong Natt has definitely done a bit of dabbling in the adult porn industry.

Also being overlooked, or at least not mentioned, is the nude photography work that Chanapa has also done and that is widely circulated on the Internet. These still photographs were obviously not meant for distribution in Thailand since they show her fully nude. (Full nudity showing the genitalia is illegal in Thailand, either to produce or distribute.)

The Thai edition of the men's magazine *Penthouse* walks a fine line in Thailand, publishing only "above the waist" full nudity, or only "implied full nudity" with none of the lower bits at all visible or facing the camera. Even so, some campaigners still set their sights on the magazine occasionally, leading to police busting vendors whilst having camera crews conveniently accompanying them. In most cases, though, the conservative side of the public are satiated that the police are doing their job, and things usually return to normal after a few short days.

One local photographer for *Penthouse* was particularly displeased by the Nong Natt pornography scandal. He'd had a photo shoot penciled in with her only weeks before the story broke in August, and had to cancel in the wake of the scandal. "Imagine how well those photos would have done?! Either locally in *Penthouse* or in overseas markets if the story had held for a few more weeks," the photographer lamented over beers with me.

Chanapa's agent had seen fit to cancel all sexually suggestive work following the scandal.

February 2005—Stepping Up

Chanapa finally appeared to answer a summons at the Crime Suppression Division's head office, a reiteration of earlier summons. In what has become Nong Natt's style in handling the media to her favor, she did not fail to impress during this round of the saga.

Police say they have evidence to support the charges against Chanapa, who says she was forced to star in the videos. Her name appeared in the credits and police hope to press charges against the other people involved (the Japanese actor(s) and producers), if they can identify them based upon information from Chanapa, if she provides it.

Chanapa dodged reporting to police for months for indecency charges relating to the pornography film.

She excelled in drawing media attention to the affair of answering the charges by showing up with her "girlfriend". In the latest account in a Thai-language tabloid, she also gave details about her relationship with her *tom* girlfriend. (A *tom* is what local Thais call a masculine lesbian, after the English word "tomboy".)

"We have been together for three years," Chanapa told local media. "And we always go out together so boys never hit on me."

And so the tawdry tale of the Thai entertainer turned porn star continues to entertain the masses as the public waits for the next twist in this saga.

After finally answering charges and paying the statutory fine—THB4,000 (US$120)—Chanapa said she wanted to move on. The fine almost seems silly given the extensive media coverage the story received, not to mention the extra attention and subsequent work that followed that, by her own accounts, has netted her hundreds of thousands of baht.

On a recent night out I was pitched to buy membership to a high-end health club, where some were citing the fact that celebrities were given free membership (and no doubt a promotional fee) to show up. Scanning the list I couldn't help noticing Natt Chanapa's name.

"Nong Natt comes here?" I asked the sales representative with a level of surprise. (Nude Thai models Nancy Ho and Irene Fah were on the list too, by the way.)

"Oh yes! At least once a week," he confirmed with a wry smile, knowing full well why a *farang* would know the name Nong Natt.

I recognized one of the PGs (promotional girls, but hardly PG in the Western sense) was actually none other than Irene Fah. She was wearing a spandex ensemble that accentuated her natural, gifted bust and pert behind as she handed out flyers and posed for pictures. When she met my gaze, the effect was immediate; maybe it was my slack-jawed inference of having seen this beauty naked and masturbating online that made it so obvious, but I am not sure who blushed more: me as the wayward *farang*, or her as a softcore model (she doesn't do hardcore). She realized immediately that I had seen her pictures and recognized her. She was nice, handed me a brochure, and then posed for an impromptu picture with me—I was the stunned "deer in the headlights", and her "headlights" are nice, I can assure you.

I managed to get her phone number, but that's a story for another day. The salesman had returned and was pushing his product.

"We don't give out regular schedules publicly; some of the celebrities don't have them anyway. But if you want to know when Nong Natt is usually here—or if she is here—we can provide that information to interested individual members privately."

The cunning salesman then added, "To provide it publicly would create a problem, you understand, and they wouldn't want to come then."

It appears there may be hope yet for me to get healthy. Although I spent more time staring at Irene, who flirtatiously returned my glances during the sales pitch, I wondered if perhaps I could find an independent outlet for exercise? I decided to call Irene the next day.

October 2006—The Comeback

Chanapa is not going away and has resurfaced again. She is making a comeback in her native Thailand after answering charges earlier this year for appearing in a pornography production. She was featured in a set of photos with an interview in a recent tabloid *VCD Digest* scantily clad and leaving little to the imagination, but in my opinion it was tasteful. She told the Thai publication that she has landed a book deal and after that she is going to get back into modeling.

Natt was more forgiving when I stumbled upon her after she had answered the charges; she was with her girlfriend in an upper-class bar and clearly did not want male attention, let alone *farang* attention. I think she figured that I was looking for an angle leading to sex. That wasn't my intention, but I certainly wasn't adverse to such an idea. Apparently, she was.

She only gave abbreviated answers, holding her girlfriend's hand most of the time. It became obvious that she was technically bisexual. "It was an opportunity," she said. "I didn't want to do it. I needed to make money." Making money, she conveyed, forces people, women, to do things they wouldn't normally consider doing. Her female *tom* companion seemed upset by this exchange, my general presence, and more or less pressed to send me on my way.

The Thai tabloid included a saucy but non-nude photoset of the popular Thai model and actress, who charged to domestic and international fame via her widely circulated pornography film. Add to this the fact that, in some cases, her apparent bisexuality has encouraged and empowered other women to relinquish their sense of shame and act more openly about their bisexual relationships, and you could say that the saga has had a positive effect for women wanting alternative, bisexual, or lesbian relationships, bringing female alternative lifestyles to the forefront of mainstream media and pop culture.

Nong Natt said that she wants to do some modeling work to show that she still has it, and then after that she wants to get into another line of work. Some speculate that she will never be able to enter mainstream modeling or entertainment, yet Thailand seems more forgiving. Thailand has watched this saucy tale with rapt attention.

In terms of the media and entertainment industry, it appears Nong Natt will feature prominently for years to come.

Now, where was that number I had for Irene Fah?

Compiled reporting, August 2004 to October 2006

Indecent exposure
in Indonesia

Indonesia, with an estimated population of over 230 million, is the world's largest Muslim nation. As such, a morality debate has intensified in recent years regarding access to sexually explicit material, specifically as more people gain access to the Internet. Perceptions of so-called Western indulgence and moral decay have alarmed many Indonesians.

In the introduction to *Jakarta Post* journalist Maggie Tiojakin's article "Sexual Evolution" it was written: "The end of the repressive New Order regime along with greater accessibility to information in the cyber-age has opened the floodgates of sexual experimentation in the past decade. While not everybody is doing it, at least they are talking about it."

Recently, Indonesian media has also reported a number of scandals involving the Internet distribution of pornographic photos of local celebrities, including a Parliament member and ordinary citizens caught in the act on camera.

In December 2006 a video began circulating the country via the Internet of lawmaker Yahya Zaini and his mistress, local pop music singer Maria Eva. While the video seemed to titillate one section of the public, Islamic leaders and moralists were less than pleased and urged the government to take action.

The Indonesian government has been quick to act, and this week announced a plan to outlaw Internet pornography. Jakarta's campaign is the latest of many developing nations which have sought to curb the allegedly damaging effects of "adult" pictures, videos, and chat rooms.

On March 25, the Indonesian government passed a law banning the accessing and production of "immoral content" on the Internet. The law, which will come into effect on March 29, is one of the strictest in the world regarding adult content: a person found guilty faces six years in prison and a fine of one billion rupiah (US$110,000).

In rapid response, a group of local hackers took over an Indonesian government website for several hours to protest against the new ban, the Information Ministry said on Friday. According to an Agence France Presse (AFP) report, "The protesters posted a message Thursday on the Ministry of Information's website challenging it to 'prove that the law was not drafted to cover the government's stupidity'."

"The message seemed to be directed at the law that was just passed by Parliament," ministry official Ferdinandus Setu told AFP, adding that the site was taken down for a period but is now back to normal.

Interestingly, the law—ostensibly aimed at protecting the moral virtue of the young generation—coincides with another government plan to extend free Internet access to all high schools in Indonesia. According to the plan's proponents, the move will bring the country's total number of Internet users to over 40 million. There are additional plans to extend free Internet access to even younger students.

Information Minister Muhammad Nuh said the decision to censor porn sites was deliberately taken in conjunction with the launch of the high school Internet access campaign. According to Nuh, an estimated 1 million locally produced pornographic sites, as well as all foreign sites that stipulate a minimum age of eighteen to enter, would be blocked from March 29. He added that "common sense will determine what is allowed and what isn't. We have to protect the nation, particularly the young generation."

Industry specific "blocking" software will be made available from the Information Ministry for download, officials said. For now, the software will operate from the user's computer, but there are plans to explore blocking it at the Internet Service Provider (ISP) level. David Burke, executive vice president of Telkom, the largest state telecommunications company, said blocking access to specific sites for Indonesian broadband users and those accessing the Internet through the country's two main gateways should not be difficult, but noted that there would be gaps.

"... Many Internet cafes obtain their bandwidth from satellites, which is much harder to control," said Burke. "So it's a huge job and there will always be cracks. It will depend on how much the government really wants to monitor and police this."

Blocking "immoral content" can be difficult. Australia for example, released similar software last year for parents and schools to use voluntarily. The project to create the software cost the government AUS$84 million (US$77 million), but within an hour of being released had been hacked into with a work-around by an Australian teenager.

In Thailand, at the height of the Thaksin Shinawatra government several years ago, it was rumored that "hundreds" of students worked as police informants to identify porn sites, which would then be blocked by the ISPs. However, authorities seemed intent on concentrating strictly on Thai pornography—or at least Asian pornography—because Western pornography remained fully accessible. Porn of all flavors returned with the 2006 coup as the military took control of all ISPs but now, under the new government, censorship seems to be returning.

Indonesia will now try its hand at Internet pornography censorship. In the Muslim country, controversy over "pornography" is certainly nothing new.

In April 2006, Islamic extremists in Jakarta gave the publishers of *Playboy*'s new Indonesian edition a seven-day ultimatum to pull it from shelves. Some violence, a burned office, and a few death threats later and the publisher was forced to move his office to Bali. Yet the Indonesian version of *Playboy* contained no nude photos, not even partial or implied nudity. It contained, in fact, pages that were more like fashion model spreads with attractive women. Nevertheless, the publisher was charged with distributing and profiting from indecent pictures. He was later exonerated.

Then, of course, there was the "Tiara Lestar scandal" that ended the young model's career amid angry howls in Indonesia. Lestar was featured partially and fully nude in Thai and Dutch editions of *Penthouse* and Spanish *Playboy*. The images were subsequently seen in Indonesia via the Internet, where they sparked outrage.

"This decision certainly wasn't popular in my own country. Heck, it was a huge disappointment for my parents, too. I regret that part of it. For that, I am sorry ... But being on the cover of *Playboy* can be considered the peak of any model's career," Lestar said in an interview last year. "However ... I appeared in a country that does not consider *Playboy* and nudity as taboo. My appearance was never intended for consumption in Indonesia. My pictures circulating on the Internet happened without my being consulted. Not offending my countrymen was one of the criteria of my decision-making process in appearing in [them]."

Lestar, it seems, didn't know much about the Internet or realize that the shots would inevitably get circulated via the Internet. One might say that Lestar even agrees with the government: she loathes Internet porn as it was the medium that allowed her nude modeling to get back to Indonesia.

Meanwhile, as Indonesia steps up its battle against online porn, some government ministers and Islamic hardliners seem to be overlooking the fact that Indonesia, like most Southeast Asian nations, has a bustling sex trade. From karaoke parlors, to hostess clubs, to bars with working girls, what's on offer within the sex trade is vast and diverse, and caters to foreigners and locals alike.

So with all this outcry and legislation against "indecency"—even of the decidedly "softcore" variety like *Playboy*—one begins to wonder what the real problem is. In the world's most populous Muslim nation, it seems that gazing at scantily clad and half-naked bar girls—and having sex with them—is OK, but looking at pictures of people doing it on the Internet is a legal issue that could land you in jail.

First published March 28, 2008 in *Asia Times Online*

Thai go-go dancer becomes a porn star

Once, there was a stunning Thai go-go dancer who was the undisputed superstar and alpha-female of Rainbow 1 in Nana Plaza. She has now found a new career. Her name is Mot, and Mango Sauce reader Jim met her back in 1999.

A veteran of over sixty visits to Thailand, Jim believes that Mot is the prettiest girl he's ever seen and a genuinely nice person too—an unlikely combination that probably renders her unique in the industry.

Sadly, just twenty-four hours after Jim took his keepsake photo, Mot was hit by a car and seriously injured. It was another six months before she could return to her chromium pole at Rainbow 1.

The physical scars had largely healed, but Jim sensed that her old confidence was gone. She told him: "I no more beautiful" and confided that she would now do "anything" to make money.

A few months later, Mot vanished from the scene and Jim lost touch with her. Recently, however, he spotted her again on a softcore pornography website called 88square.com. The photographers from 88square.com work almost exclusively with Thai models. Now going by the name Vivian Lin (and occasionally Petchara) she has, it seems, embarked upon a glittering new career as a porn star.

Good career move?

Some would argue that entering the porn industry might not be the best career choice. However, in Mot's case it would seem that working as a model for adult pictures is better than working as a go-go-dancing prostitute.

Prostitution in Thailand is illegal; so is porn. Still, both are almost systematically overlooked by the Thai authorities. A recent case highlighted this issue when Natt Chanapa was summoned by the Thai police for her appearance in a hardcore porn movie (it should also be noted that Chanapa has also been photographed by the 88square.com photographers).

Just as the Thai police tend to overlook prostitution, they also seem to allow nude modeling and photography to slide by. It was Natt's appearance in the movie that caused the uproar, not the many nude photo shoots she had done, so Mot may be safe in her new career. Add to this the fact that Natt was also already a mainstream model and actress before the porn tape surfaced, and it is easy to see how it became an issue.

Moreover, one must consider the perils of working in the sex industry as a prostitute. Foremost would be the chances of contracting sexually transmitted diseases. But other dangers rear their ugly heads from time to time—the worst stories are of girls being beaten by customers and even killed.

The emotional toll on the women in the sex industry can't be overlooked either. While almost all girls in Thailand's sex industry enter it "voluntarily", it is only due to financial hardship and limited career options that the women are "forced" into this career. Add to this the stress of having sex with strangers, who can sometimes be abusive, and it is easy to see why these women sink into depression.

Sabai, sabai

Mot's career in pornography has afforded her a more comfortable lifestyle financially. Gone are the long nights gyrating away on a stage till 1 am for drunken middle-aged sex tourists. So, too, is the requirement for her to go with these same customers for sex. Photo shoots and modeling jobs are more likely to happen during normal working hours and are certainly more comfortable for her than the aforementioned work. So all in all, it could be a job that could bring her international stardom, a relatively long-term paying career, and keep her safe from the perils of Thailand's prostitution industry.

September 2005, A Top Model

First reported as Vivian Lin (a.k.a Mot, Petchara, and Wong Sze Ka to push her in the Chinese market), this girl has been making waves as a top Internet model, and in 2004 was voted Surfers' Choice Model at Asian4You, taking 41% of the final tally of thousands of votes.

But the fledgling adult model has also garnered mainstream film roles in Thailand's movie industry, playing a supporting role in *She's Ann*, starring none other than Natt Chanapa (a.k.a Kesarin Chaichalermpol, Natt Kesarin, or simply Nong Natt). *She's Ann* tells the story of an ordinary woman who leaves her boyfriend to pursue a relationship with another man in the hope of a better life. But the plan goes awry, and the title character Ann (played by Chanapa) ends up in the sex industry instead. Lin plays a supporting role to Chanapa as a friend she meets in the sex industry.

Asian Sex Gazette's early coverage of the film drew international attention and criticism alike, as we were the first to report the scandal in English-based on translations of Thai reports. ASG pointed out that Lin had previously worked in Thailand's sex industry, making far less than she does as a model and now actress.

The change of careers happened by accident—literally. While Lin was still employed in the sex industry, she was badly injured one night by a hit-and-run driver. As she was recovering, she took stock of her life, and when her beauty caught the eye of a local adult photographer from 88Square.com, who presented her with a modeling opportunity, she gave up sex work.

Some took issue with ASG's early reporting, saying Lin was giving up one form of exploitation for another.

Asian Sex Gazette stands by our original report that contends she went from one form of voluntary sex work to adult modeling and now mainstream acting—and that the latest career is arguably one in which she is at less risk of exploitation, trafficking, and/or sexually transmitted diseases. She had been recognized for her modeling beauty—even if it was an adult form of modeling.

Lin's recovery was not easy. And it has not been made easier by those pundits contemplating her level of morality within the differing views of Thai society and beyond. By and large, the photos of this stunning vixen are beyond the fragile lines of Thai law because they show genitalia, which is forbidden. However, this level of the law is rarely enforced in still softcore pornography photos, not against the models at least. Photographers and producers, especially if they're foreign, are not so lucky in the eyes of the law.

Yet as we have witnessed recently, the Thai authorities, in their ever-increasing war on "dark influence", seem increasingly keen to prosecute and demonize those women who make the decision to involve themselves in the adult industry.

Unlike her co-star and buddy Nong Natt, Lin seems to have thus far avoided close scrutiny and prosecution by the authorities. This is despite the fact that some of her more recent adult industry work has included solo masturbation video clips, with and without utilizing sex toys, which is certainly pushing the card as far as what the Thai authorities find acceptable.

Compiled reporting, August 2004 to September 2005
MangoSauce.com and *Asian Sirens* contributed to this report.

The Philippines
exports labor and sex

Although prostitution is illegal in the Philippines, sex remains a thriving industry, both domestically and abroad. Many Filipinas ply the world's oldest profession in an attempt to overcome crushing poverty and the oppressive economic crisis gripping their homeland. Even Filipinas who work overseas legally—as maids, nannies, entertainers, nurses, or in other legitimate occupations—often find themselves turning to the sex trade to supplement meager incomes and to send money home to the Philippines to support impoverished family members.

The Philippines has a bustling sex trade with much variety. Small bars and clubs serve locals—often taxi drivers, laborers, and even local teenagers looking to solve their virginity issues—and employ women from poor rural areas who "service" clients for as little as 200–400 pesos (US$5–$10). More glitzy establishments cater to foreigners, especially in areas such as Makati, Pasay, Ermita, or Angeles City, where Guest Relations Officers (GROs) can charge as much as 2,000–3,000 pesos (US$50–$75), even for a short-time experience.

A recent visit to Makati, the business district of Manila, found bars packed with scantily clad girls, many adorned in thong bikinis or lingerie, and gyrating enthusiastically to Western pop music. Several were equally enthusiastically grinding their nearly naked bodies against male customers in the hope of enticing a business arrangement. The enticement is obviously doubled when two girls set upon a customer, but the 5,000 pesos (US$150) or so required to take them out can have a cooling effect.

More "off the beaten track" places can be found throughout the Philippines, especially any place catering to foreign tourists, which is just about everywhere. Prices in these venues range from 1,000–2,000 pesos (US$25–$50), but the price tag is often enough for an overnight companion.

Prices aside, the sheer volume of sex workers in the Philippines is staggering. The most recent report, but sadly outdated, by the International Labor Organization (ILO) estimated that as of 1998 there were as many 500,000 women working in the sex trade.

The ILO report also estimated that some 150,000 Filipinas were working in Japan as "entertainers". In a 2005 interview with the *Philippine Star,* a woman explained the realities of working there: "I used to work in Japan. I was there only six months. We enter as entertainers, but most of us have to earn through prostitution."

The Japanese Government was placed in Tier 2 in the 2007 US Department of State's *Trafficking in Persons Report* for not fully complying with the Trafficking Victims Protection Act's minimum standards for the elimination of trafficking, but making "significant efforts" to do so. Japan's significant effort appears to be largely based on a few arrests and limiting the number of entertainer's visas to between about 80,000 and 100,000.

The Philippine government's own policies regarding overseas contract workers (OCWs) only help to encourage the flow of women working abroad. But the situation in Japan is hardly unique: the popularity of Filipina OCWs is also evident on any Sunday afternoon on the streets and in the parks of Hong Kong. As Sunday is traditionally a day off for OCWs, hundreds of thousands of Filipinas meet to socialize with their compatriots.

While many work as household helpers, a visit to Wan Chai, Hong Kong's red-light district, makes it obvious that some Filipinas are moonlighting in the sex trade.

One such woman told Asia Times Online that she was a domestic helper, but frequented clubs to sell sex to mostly expatriate clients. "Yeah, I come to the bars sometimes to look for some extra cash from the customers for short-time sex. In just a couple of hours, a few days a week, I can easily double my salary," said the twenty-three-year-old, who added that she was lucky to work for an employer who let her come out a few times a week.

"Some girls only get to come out on Sundays; it is not as easy for them. Even then, some have strict curfews from their bosses. One girl had an ex-employer who would only let her out on Sundays, and then she had to be back by 7 pm. When the girl asked the employer why, the boss said, 'If you go out to the bars, you'll get pregnant and then I'll have to find a new maid.' Can you imagine that?" she said.

"If nothing else, I can see some friends and have a beer, maybe get lucky and make some money. It is always good when the US fleet is in town; I have had as many as three customers in one night," she added, appearing truly pleased by her good fortune.

"I want to send money back to my family in the Philippines and save some for myself. I don't get much as a maid so this helps me earn more," she said as she placed her hand on my thigh.

The standard government-dictated minimum wage for a domestic helper is HK$3,480 (US$450) per month, plus housing—but I have never met a maid who made more than the minimum. So working the bars can mean serious income for girls who charge usually a minimum of HK$1,000 (US$128) for a quickie.

The situation for underpaid domestic helpers is consistent across Asia; not just in Hong Kong, but also in Singapore,

Australia, and Malaysia. From Shanghai to Dubai, young Asian women, frequently Filipinas, end up featuring prominently in the local sex scene.

The international migration of Filipinos seeking work has been prominent for decades. In the Philippines, labor is the top export; the government has long encouraged the practice by offering assistance in getting overseas jobs. One such perk is that OCWs are given "first grab" for prime land purchases in certain areas in the Philippines, with mortgages being subsidized by the government at low interest rates.

Asia Times Online reported last month that the country's central bank estimated that migrant workers sent home at least US$14 billion in 2007, almost a billion dollars more than the global pornography industry. This makes the Philippines number three in the world for foreign remittances, behind only Mexico and India. Each year funds sent from abroad represent almost 10% of the country's annual GDP.

It is hard to calculate exactly, but a portion of the money sent home is no doubt coming from exporting Filipinas not only for labor, but also for sex.

First published March 15, 2008 in *Asia Times Online*

Getting your fill
in the Philippines

The plane deposited us unceremoniously at Ninoy Aquino International Airport in Manila on a steamy late afternoon to join throngs of people, some lumbering toward immigration, others moving about randomly, and still more waiting and keeping physical movement to a minimum, perhaps to limit the effect of the oppressive heat. My friend and I finally got through immigration, found a taxi, and were on our way on what we had dubbed a "boy's holiday" in the sultry Philippine Islands.

We were dropped in a rather plain, nondescript area on P. Burgos Street in Makati, Metro Manila, and checked into our hotel. After getting settled, we met after an hour or so to get something to eat. Making our way down the streets to find dinner it became clear that, as dusk fell, a transformation in Makati was occurring. A few random touts offered to sell us Viagra, and neon started to glow from what had appeared to be innocuous pubs during the day.

We settled on a small pub restaurant where the menu consisted of standard Spanish-inspired Philippine fare. Tasty tapas, grilled chicken, and rice complemented by a few San Miguel beers rounded off our first meal of local flavor. Then it was time to hit the town.

My mate had done most of the planning for the trip as he had been there previously, and he explained that he had chosen

Makati as it is home to one of the main red-light districts. Indeed, as we emerged into the now dark streets after dinner, this became obvious. The transformation was now complete. Booming music escaped from some of the clubs we passed, touts were out in force, and sexy, suggestive neon signs were everywhere.

We picked a go-go bar and took the plunge. Even though there were only a dozen or so girls there, with half of them dancing on a small stage at the back of the bar, we decided to stay on for a bit as it was a good starting point. Drinks in hand, we chatted and took in the flirtatious girls as they danced. We were just about the only customers.

As it turned out, I was later glad we'd decided to stay because though it took me a few moments to notice her, there was a stunning young Filipina dancing in a thong bikini and she was damn near perfect. There is something about the super-petite women that Asia offers that has always caught my fancy. This girl probably weighed about 100 lbs (45 kgs) soaking wet, with ample C-cup cleavage, a washboard stomach, Spanish hips, and surprisingly long, toned legs. In fact, she was probably about five feet four (163 cm), which is quite statuesque in my opinion for Asian women—of course, this was added to by the platform heels she was wearing that probably gave her another five to six inches (13–15cm).

Even after a moment or two of bewildered staring, a consummate professional does not fail to notice a major catch. And though the dancing beauty was too involved in her dance performance to notice me, the stunned customer, the effect was not lost on the *mamasan*, who immediately called the girl off stage and had her sit with me. Life was good.

Drinks were bought and I chatted with the girl, which is easy with Filipinas because of their English skills—quite a bit easier than chatting up Thai girls. My mate seemed to have similarly attracted the attention and company of another girl, so I was happy to find he was being entertained too. Mine told me her name was Faith, she was nineteen years old, and had been working in the bar for only a few months. I suppressed a shudder.

She gave me the standard story: poor family, crippling poverty, need to make money. A departure from the standard Thai-style mantra, though, was that she was hoping to make enough money to get herself on the foreign "entertainers" circuit, singing or dancing at clubs in Japan, Hong Kong, or Singapore. Such "entertainment" visas are, in many cases, a cover for prostitution.

When queried about barfines and fees for her entertainment services for the evening, she seemed taken aback. "I don't go with customers! I earn money from dancing and having customers buy me drinks. No sex! I am a virgin!"

Again bewildered, I suppressed a shudder, though I had trouble believing her story.

Sensing my disbelief, she suddenly offered to show me her ID to confirm that she had in fact just turned nineteen and hadn't been working in the bar long. "I'll show you my ID card if you want. I just turned nineteen last month," she persisted.

I told her it wouldn't be necessary and that I believed her. Yet she still flirted, stroked my thigh, and brushed her perky breasts against me—not quite in the uninhibited and sexually suggestive ways I have found in seasoned bar girls in Bangkok and beyond, but the girl knew the moves.

An intermission in my confusion finally arrived when the girls my companion and I were fawning over and buying drinks for were suddenly summoned to dance, leaving us alone.

"Gorgeous girl, what's her story?" my friend asked.

"I don't know," I said, still confused. "Says she doesn't go with customers, nineteen, claims to be a virgin … I don't know."

After a winning smirk and sigh of confidence, my mate said with a laugh. "You just met your first 'cherry girl'."

"Cherry girls are 'virgins', at least in terms of the sex trade, or so they claim," he explained. "When you get them back to your room and have sex and realize they are not physically virgins, the claim will be that you are the first 'customer' they have gone with, thus they were a 'virgin' to the sex industry. Of course, if a guy is not smart enough to know the difference, the 'I'm a real virgin' thing will hold as their story."

"Congratulations!" he beamed. "First cherry girl!"

"I don't understand," I said. "How does she make money? Not just from dancing and drinks?" I could not see how working in such an environment, paying bills, and facing the demands imposed on a sex worker who doesn't have sex could support a cherry girl adequately.

"Of course not," my friend confirmed. "She is a 'cherry girl'. That means you have to initiate aggressive bidding. There is no barfine, short-time, or long-time/overnight rate for her—it is what someone is willing to pay for her 'cherry'."

"The young, fresh girls get away with it," he continued. "Thailand—or rather the girls and *mamasans* there—have rarely gotten so clever as to employ such tactics. But as you already know, the younger, fresher, and prettier girls in Thailand can command a higher basic price."

"So you can take her? She is just playing hard to get?" I asked him.

"Oh, you can take her, but plan on spending at least 10,000 pesos (US$230) base. Probably a lot more for her," he added, marveling at her beauty and sexuality much as I had done. "It is a bidding war. They'll make you feel like you are offering some paltry amount, even at the inflated price. Hell, if you offered 50,000 pesos (US$1,140) they'd probably still find a way to make

67

you feel that this was an inadequate amount. Cherry girls are nice, but not nice to pay for. Let's move on."

I followed my comrade in arms to the next bar. There was something different about these go-go bars compared to those in Thailand or Hong Kong. Finally, I was able to define it: the girls liked dancing. Whereas Thai go-go girls are hit or miss dancewise, these Filipinas danced with enthusiasm. In fact, when a song came on that the girls seemed to particularly like, they would even break into some little sexy choreographed routine. Filipinas, I concluded, are quite good at the dancing part of the go-go trade.

In Thailand, by contrast, the best you can usually hope for in terms of good dancing is just a sexy stripper-styled routine and pole grinding by a girl who seems to be dancing to her own tune.

After having a drink or two in a series of these dance-style go-go bars, we settled on one near our hotel that had some particularly cute girls and good uniforms—lingerie that left little to the imagination. It was at this fine establishment that I was accosted by two lovely girls determined to ensure that I wouldn't want to leave alone.

One was dressed in a red-lace garter, stockings, G-string, and bra, while the other was in a simpler, though sheer, white bra and thong. A winning combination, in my opinion. What was a bit surprising was the aggressive manner in which these women pursued their goal, at times nearly pinning me down and rubbing various bits of themselves over parts of me. Not that this was completely objectionable, mind you.

Lady in Red's hair was in pigtails, while Thong Girl's hair hung loosely down her back, but both boasted long locks. Fine, tanned, golden-brown skin, dark eyes, and pouting full lips on Lady in Red plus ample cleavage; Thong Girl was less endowed breastwise, but she had high, prominent cheekbones and long legs which added to her beauty.

My friend was also enjoying some company, but the girl entertaining him seemed much more laid-back and simply chatted while they groped each other.

These girls though, my God, a barrel of monkeys! One had her crotch in my face, flashing her pussy, while the other was grinding her pelvis on my lap. Suddenly the one "in my face" flipped, somehow, into a quasi-69 seated position and ground her muff on my chin while her friend had also repositioned herself, playfully pretending to lick her friend's vagina. Moments later, the girls were sitting on my lap kissing and licking each other's nipples and stroking my cock through my shorts. I couldn't keep track of them!

"Having a good time?" my buddy shouted over the music, laughing.

"They're out of control!" I said, flabbergasted and coming up for air. I heard a roar of laughter as my view of him was blocked by a pair of breasts.

This continued for a while until I began visualizing headlines like "Sex columnist killed in ménage à trois in Philippines". Finally, they began to let up a bit.

"I have to go to the bathroom, you'll wait for me?" Lady in Red asked, and Thong Girl chimed in, "You'll buy drinks for us?"

"Yes, yes, go to the bathroom! I'll wait! And you," I said to Thong Girl, "get drinks, something strong for God's sake. Buy drinks! Buy tranquilizers!" I told them, and they pranced off together.

"You keeping entertained? I don't want you to get bored or anything," my friend said sarcastically.

I glared at him. "So much for demure Catholic girls then, eh?"

"Listen, the prices seem to have gone up recently," he said.

"I don't know how much the members of The Philippines' National Acrobatic Team are asking for, but this girl is saying 500 pesos (US$11) barfine and 2,000 pesos (US$45) for her," he said, indicating the young lady sitting beside him, oblivious to our conversation with the booming music.

As we'd planned a boat trip the next morning, we decided we'd cut it short after a few more drinks and be good boys on the first night of our boy's holiday.

"Anyway, I guess we'll chat more later—your acrobats are coming back," he said, nodding his head in their direction.

I wondered to myself if the adrenaline surge had anything to do with the basic animal instinct of fight or flight. But sitting there, decidedly not getting up, and watching the two beauties approach, I knew it was another basic animal instinct ruling the day: an erection.

With a lot of work, I was able to get them to seat themselves on either side of me and mildly behave. This was hard work, mind you; while getting the one on the right to get her hand out of my pants, the one on the left would start licking and nibbling my ear. Turning to stop her would have the one on the right again attacking my zipper or biting my nipples.

I managed to ask their names, and Lady in Red told me she was Anna and the girl currently kissing me on the neck to the right (Thong Girl) was Ann.

"Easy, right? And you don't have to worry about it in bed; you can always say you were screaming out 'Ann! Anna! Ann uh!'" Anna said with a giggle.

Chastising Ann momentarily and distracting her with a drink, I tried picking up the conversation with her.

"So, do you and Anna go with customers together a lot?" I asked, noting that Anna had taken to groping my crotch now.

"Only when we like the same man," Ann said quite seductively, and proceeded to rub her breasts against my chest as she kissed me full on the lips.

I enquired about how much it would cost me for them to go with me for the evening, and wasn't necessarily surprised when Ann told me 1,000 pesos (US$22) for the bar and 2,500 pesos (US$55) each. Meanwhile, Anna had gotten into my pants again and I suddenly felt the very distinct, and enjoyable, sensation of oral sex.

"Hey, stop that!" I said, turning and pulling her off me as she smiled mischievously. "A guy needs a tranquilizer gun to deal with you two."

It was time to make for the exit, and I signaled to my friend, who concurred. I tried to excuse myself from the girls but they weren't having any of it. Some guys might have gotten angry about all this, which would have sent the girls scurrying, but I was trying to handle the situation in good spirits and with humor. The whole time the girls were begging me not to go, or to at least take them with me. Their price dropped to 2,000 pesos (US$45) each in the process, then 1,500 pesos (US$35).

I made my way to the door with them hanging off of me, and one of them—I think it was Anna—nearly body-tackled me. I didn't go down, but in her grasp and the melee of confusion, I failed to notice one of them had managed to unfasten a button on my shorts, which was exacerbated by the fact that my fly was still halfway down from Anna's last attempt to accost me, threatening to leave me with my shorts around my ankles. (I go "commando", in case you are wondering, which would have made this especially bad.)

This only fanned the flames of the fire, inciting whoops from other bar girls and even a few patrons who were getting a kick out of the impromptu show. By the time I made it to the door and out of their grasp, I stumbled, tripping almost flat on my face trying to keep my pants halfway on. My mate was already outside and almost doubled over in laughter.

"Yeah, very funny," I said, righting myself and securing my pants. "Remind me to bring a Taser if we come back here."

The Next Island

At sea, the formidable heat was mitigated by the ocean breeze, and as we motored along I couldn't help appreciating the beauty and tranquility of a sea voyage in Southeast Asia. The destination was Puerto Galera, a comparatively sleepy little island community that we had chosen for exactly that reason.

Arriving at Sabang Beach, we were pleased to find that the hotel we had pre-booked was about a city-block trek down the beach from the boat's landing spot—not that there was anything urban about the place. It was a tropical getaway; a paradise. There weren't the usual city comforts and facilities for a hundred miles—not even ATMs (believe me, I know).

The ensuing six days and five nights were not lacking in debauchery, drinking and, fortunately, relaxing. We sought out no local sights, and instead took part in a completely sedentary style of tourism: wake up midday, get some food, find justification for an early beer, maybe dinner, then off to the bars. Hey, I could claim I was working, right?

For such a small place, it was a pretty decent tourist destination. This makes prostitution an inevitable ingredient in the mix, but considering the size of the town, the local sex industry was formidable.

On the first night we went to a little "pub" that promised live music, girls, and cold beers. I had been chatting up the *mamasan* for a few minutes when I was distracted by a hard-bodied girl who was setting up the kit for the music performance.

"Ah, you like Grace?" the *mamasan* said. "She is my daughter, eighteen, a great singer. Would you like to meet her?"

"Your daughter? Uh," I stammered. "No, it is okay. But she is beautiful," I offered as a compliment.

There was no stopping Mama though, who called over her daughter, Grace, and introduced us. Grace was polite, even seemingly taken aback that a foreigner liked her. She was shy, giggling unnecessarily. I bought her a drink, but decided I should move on—certainly no fault of Grace's, though. I just felt awkward chatting up the *mamasan*'s daughter. I didn't get to hear her sing that night.

Ending up at a go-go bar which, surprisingly, existed in this idyllic location (maybe that made it more idyllic?), I chose some girl who probably weighed 90 lbs (41kg), with nice long hair and legs, and we went home.

I awoke the next morning wondering who the Filipina strutting around naked was. What was her name? Did I need to pay her? I remembered that we had had sex the night before, but I was confused. How do these things happen? I wondered.

"C'mon, take a shower with me," she said, dropping any pretext of business. "C'mon. I have to have dinner with the girls in an hour or so." She stood naked before me, beckoning me to have sex in the shower with her. Who was I to refuse?

By the Grace of God

Somehow I ended up at Grace's bar again—her singing was great, by the way. I don't know how—drinks were involved—but she came back with me to the hotel.

Much to my consternation, she refused sex with a condom. Filipinas, most of whom are Catholic, have the unfortunate disadvantage in the realm of sexual health and education that the Catholic Church does not condone the use of condoms; sex is for procreation, between a husband and wife, and any other sex is sinful. So condoms, which imply sex is for pleasure and not procreation, are simply unacceptable.

Grace also refused to allow me to pay her, saying she was not like that, not viewing herself as a working girl. She said I could buy her drinks at the bar, which apparently she got a commission for, and watch her show. So that is exactly what I did for the next few nights, but purposely not taking her every night as I didn't want to seem to be taking advantage. While this was going on, the *mamasan*—who took great pleasure in me calling her "Mama"—began doting on me, offering a free drink every few drinks and occasionally inviting me to join the bar staff and musicians in the corner and snack on Filipino food.

It was a good time and I was happy to be included. My friend and I sometimes went out together, but he had found his own haunts of particular (female) interest, which was fine for both of us.

The last night finally arrived and I again spent the evening at Grace's bar watching and, of course, shared her company back at the hotel. She said she was sad I was leaving but did not get very emotional about it, explaining simply, "This is a tourist resort. People come and people go."

Indeed I could not imagine what it must have been like for her growing up in such an environment. She said she was happy and enjoyed performing, and felt she was getting better all the time—which I found impressive because I already felt she was quite good. She too said that she would like to get an entertainer's visa, but unlike Faith back in Manila, she wanted to go through the country's entertainer-certification process.

The Philippines has a process in place where Filipinos wanting to work overseas as entertainers apply and are evaluated on their skill and performance, then, if deemed skilled enough, are approved and the government certifies them as performers. They are then added to the list of entertainers and pushed by agents to resorts and clubs across Asia, and around the world for that matter, to perform. The Filipinos' natural skills in English as a second language make them a nearly unchallenged entertainment commodity at resorts catering to Westerners. The aim is also to mitigate human trafficking for prostitution by fake entertainers seeking visas.

Back in the Big City

We arrived back in Manila after a trip that seemed much longer and grinding on the spirit than the outbound trip had been. Eager to make the most of our last few days, we didn't let this slow us down. My friend felt a change of location was in order and, always being good at research, decided that the Ermita district was appropriate.

We found a reasonably priced hotel called Amazonia. I couldn't help giggling over the fact that we were staying in a hotel that had a half-go-go, half-pub-style venue in the ground-floor lobby. Convenient, I thought to myself. The girls changed uniforms each day: one day they were cowgirls complete with cowboy hats, cutoff denim hot pants, and micro Western button-down shirts tied off in a knot at the midsection, and the next they were uniformed Catholic schoolgirls with their hair tied in pigtails. Apparently there was also a law-enforcement day that we didn't have the pleasure of being present for.

The place also served food, had pool tables, darts and so forth, so to call it strictly a pick-up joint or go-go bar would be unfair, but it certainly was a place you could deem as "full service". But as it turned out, I did not end up needing or considering the girls' full services.

Checked in and settled, we headed out for an afternoon beer, walking a few blocks to a bar called LA Cafe that, upon entering, one immediately realizes is a freelance bar—and surprisingly busy considering it was mid-afternoon. We found a table, ordered beers, and chatted while taking in the sights the bar had to offer.

It wasn't long, of course, until a girl approached the table and introduced herself as Maggie (no doubt short for Magdalene—such wonderful reliance on good Catholic names). Beer in hand, she asked if she and her friend could join us. She was obviously interested in me. I was indifferent as she wasn't particularly beautiful; cute, yes, but she unfortunately had bad teeth, which is a turnoff for me. Then I noticed her friend who was trailing along behind her lackadaisically. Damn, I thought to myself.

"Sure, have a seat!" I said, my mood suddenly brightening. My buddy eyed me suspiciously; he knows me too well.

Maggie was from … somewhere, and mentioned some other … stuff. She was nice, don't get me wrong, but her friend was a hottie. I was even more intrigued by her standoffish position—both physically, the way she seated herself, and her interaction. She was warm and friendly, but didn't take up the default position of a sex worker alongside my buddy, as most seeking a customer do. We all chatted, bought beers for the ladies, and had a very good time. At one point Maggie's friend, who I learned was named Mary, seemed to notice my glances, but was unfazed by the attention.

Mary was more full-figured than the starved-catwalk-model-style girls I usually like. By no means was she fat, just curvy, kind of a Filipina version of J-Lo. The effect was quite positive, I can assure you. Busty at the front with a backside that was screaming to be fondled, she wore no make-up—or maybe a minimal amount (I am a guy, remember, so I don't know)—yet was naturally beautiful and demure.

She was dressed in a casual fashion, nothing overly sexy or seeking to attract attention, unlike other girls or her friend Maggie, which in a way made her even more alluring. I decided she could have been wearing a burlap rice sack and still look sexy.

Eventually, we decided to change bars, and my friend was keen to get something to eat, so we decided to go back to the hotel. Maggie asked if we wanted her to come with us. An impasse was reached: "Did Mary want to come too?" I asked. Mary seemed a bit taken aback, but said that she would.

Walking back to Amazonia, my buddy angled to get alongside me while the girls walked together chatting in Tagalog. "You're going to try to pull a switch, aren't you?"

"Yeah," I said simply, knowing this can be a dangerous, fruitless effort.

"Good luck, she's worth it," he answered.

Back at Amazonia, drinks and food were ordered and we took to playing pool. My cohort drew the attention of one of the Amazonia girls who on this day were dressed as schoolgirls, and she happily joined us, making me happy that he had company while I played out my own personal soap opera.

While I was playing pool with Maggie, she initiated the "end game", and propositioned me about being my companion for the evening. It was now or never. As cautiously and gently as possible, I told her that I thought she was a very nice and attractive girl, but that I was interested in Mary, and for that reason it wouldn't be right for me to take her, as I would be thinking of Mary. I apologized, and she seemed to take it better than I expected.

"Do you think Mary would be interesting in staying with me?" I asked, and she surprised me by taking on the role of matchmaker for a guy who, in essence, had just jilted her.

"I don't know, let me ask her," she said, walking over to the table where Mary was sitting with a beer, picking at some food we had ordered. When Maggie pulled her aside and started telling her my proposition, I could tell Mary was taken by surprise. She blushed and smiled a bit, which made her even cuter, and I felt it was a good sign. When she glanced over at me, I pretended not to be paying attention, and instead looked around aimlessly.

Maggie returned a few minutes later with a confident smile, and I was hopeful. Indeed, Mary had said she would hang out for the evening, but there were conditions. First, Maggie advised that sex was not automatic—which I found to be rather blunt—but play my cards right, and who knows? Second, I would have to give Maggie 1,000 pesos (US$22) for taking up her time when she could have been finding a real customer. Fair enough, I thought. "Be good to her, she is a friend for a long time, we went to school together," Maggie said, adding that she was going back to LA Cafe. She made her exit after talking with Mary for a moment. I noticed my friend casting quizzical glances between the girls and me. When Maggie turned to him and said goodbye then made for the door while Mary remained, he looked over at me with a raised brow and a silent but knowing smile.

I made for the table where my friend was, sat down, and ordered another drink for myself and anyone else who needed one. To say that there was an awkward silence for a few moments would be putting it mildly. After giving me a look of approval, my friend made a point of becoming deeply involved in a conversation with his girl and pretended that we didn't exist.

"I had no idea you felt this way," Mary said. "I guess I have gotten rusty."

"Sorry, I didn't mean to make anyone feel uncomfortable," I responded.

"No, it is okay. I am flattered actually. It has just been a while," she said, again with the cute blushing and smile. The last bit of her statement confused me a bit: surely a girl of her beauty would not have to wait a "while" for male attention.

This piece of the puzzle snapped into place a few minutes later when I asked the basic conversation question of where she was from, and she answered: "Chicago."

Wait, what? I'm from Chicago! Yet I could not discount what she'd said, because the way she'd said it, in a perfect Chicago accent, was confirmation in itself: "Chee-kaa-go." It was then that I realized that most of her speech was peppered with a Chicago accent.

"Chicago! I'm from Chicago!" I said. "What part of Chicago?"

"Really?" she said, perking up a bit. "North Side: Western and Damen. You?"

"State and Maple," I answered.

"Woo, look at you—'Gold Coast'," she said sarcastically. It was at this point that I realized how American her speech was, accented nicely with Midwest Chicago tones.

We got on well after suddenly discovering we had a shared thread of personal history. As the evening wore on amicably, we flirted, drank, ate, played pool, and continued chatting and learning about each other. She was from Cavite originally, she was twenty-six, met a nice American man when she was twenty, fell in love, married him, and moved to the US—Chicago. Over the past six years she had had two boys, now four and one and a half.

A few years ago, after the first baby, the relationship with her husband turned sour as he turned out to be the jealous type and would fly into a fit of anger if she so much as said hello to a male neighbor. After the second child it got worse, and she began feeling that she was living a sheltered existence. The breaking point came one day when, going to get the mail, she dropped a piece of it. A black male neighbor noticed, picked it up, called to her and handed it to her politely. She smiled, thanked him, and returned to the apartment, where apparently her husband had been watching. He flew into a rage.

He accused her of cheating on him with a "nigger" (a term she found extremely offensive: being Asian, what was she then?), but the real deal breaker came moments later when he hit her.

As a sex journalist, I can tell you that hitting a Latina—an ethnic group to which I consider Filipinas to be very close, given their cultural heritage—is a very bad idea. Of course, a man hitting a woman of any cultural variant is unacceptable, but with Latinas (and Filipinas), you are especially putting yourself in peril. Best-case scenario: the woman leaves you as a result of your unacceptable behavior. Worst-case scenario: she fights back with a stunning, no-holds-barred mantra that would impress Ultimate Fighting competitors. Mind you, UF competitors are not allowed to use weapons in competition; Filipinas and Latinas have no such limitations.

Mary's kids were staying with their father, but not for long. When her husband hit her, she called the police, who arrested the husband for domestic abuse and battery. The divorce case did not look good for him with such a history. Add to this the fact his mother had recently died, leaving behind a substantial family fortune in excess of US$7 million with him as the sole heir, and you could say he was having a bad day; but at his own doing, of course. Mary said she had a good lawyer, was pleased with US marital law, and expected to take half his assets plus alimony and child support.

"Shit, this girl is going to be a millionaire soon," I thought to myself. She was planning on moving with her kids to California, where she had family, and opening a beauty salon and supply store.

"I am going to destroy him," she said confidently, and with a degree of satisfaction. "Take half his assets, pay me every month, and make him fly halfway across the country for visitation. I win. He's an asshole."

"So why are you here?" I asked her. "With Maggie, in the freelance bars?"

"I am not here, like, for that, if that's what you mean," she replied. "I'm not a prostitute! Maggie has had bad luck, I suppose, but she does okay. I only agreed to stick around because I found you attractive, and I was flattered by the fact that you've been the first man in a long time to make a pass at me."

"Sorry, I didn't mean any disrespect," I said, frantically backpedaling. "It's just, I don't know, I guess I was just confused, meeting you and Maggie at LA Cafe and all."

"It's understandable, don't worry about it," she assured me, adding with a coy glance: "Girls want to have fun sometimes too, you know."

Fun was had indeed. We stayed together for the rest of my trip, though it was just sex, eating, bar-hopping, and drinking. Once again, like Grace, she was averse to condoms but assured me that she had a clean bill of health. "You're the first man I have been around since my husband and the kids," she said.

Also like Grace, Mary wasn't emotional when the time came for me to leave. She gave me an affectionate kiss, pressed a slip of paper with her e-mail address into my hand, and told me to take care. She waved to me as my taxi pulled away.

We kept in touch via e-mail and I learned many months later that her divorce had gone favorably, as she expected, and she was living in California as she had planned, feeling that she had gotten the happy ending she deserved.

Songkran: hard holiday for ladyboys

Songkran, the Thai New Year celebration held every April, is the world's largest water fight, when young and old, foreign and Thai alike enjoy and participate in the revelry. However, for Thailand's transsexual ladyboys (known as *katoey*s in Thai) it can be an annoying and precarious holiday.

The no-holds-barred water fights that have become part of the tradition of Songkran have their roots in early rituals that included lightly pouring water over the hands and feet of elders in a cleansing ritual. Historically, the festival also represented well-wishing and good luck, and marked the beginning of the rainy season and the hope of a productive rice crop. Nowadays, it has been joyously hijacked from a traditional, tranquil water festival to a free-for-all water fight.

For Thai ladyboys, the holiday can be a daunting gauntlet of self-preservation.

Thai transsexuals are widely accepted and often considered by their natural female counterparts to be the most beautiful "women" in Thailand. They feature widely in local media and the advertising industry. Thai men who want to become women go through a myriad of surgeries, treatments, and self-improvement procedures to make the successful leap from male to female. And the doctors that perform these procedures are some of the best sexual reassignment surgeons in the world. The number of "medical tourism" travelers who visit Thailand to benefit from the knowledge and experience of these doctors has risen. Not to mention the fact that it is much cheaper in Thailand than in the West. The procedure can be performed at reputable hospitals for as little as THB120,000 (US$3,800).

Breast augmentation, rhinoplasty, Botox injections, and hormone treatments are among the basics a guy must undertake to begin the transition. For those who take the final step, there is sexual-reassignment surgery with the necessary vaginoplasty procedure to make them "whole" as a female.

Sexual-reassignment surgery is not for the faint of heart. I watched one after making a questionable request in the spirit of journalism. I puked, I'll admit it, and had to run out of the surgery choking back stomach acid. Luckily I found a nearby toilet in time. To my credit, I did return, much to the consternation of the surgeons.

Seriously though, it's not easy watching the male penis, an organ I myself hold a strong personal affinity for, being sliced lengthwise along the underside, only to be essentially gutted, sutchered, then the flap of skin turned inside out by shoving it up into the pelvis to form the "vagina". Add to this the final coup de grâce of slicing up the scrotum and discarding some other, often treasured, male bits (think "testicles"), then using the remaining scrotal tissue to form the outer labia. Again, not for the faint of heart.

The "woman" will then have to spend the next weeks and months "masturbating" herself, gently at first, of course, with a sex toy and special sterile-lubricant mix to ensure that her vagina heals fully open so she is able to have intercourse.

Yet there is sometimes still some "fine-tuning" to perfect the lady. This may include permanent hair removal, more Botox and silicon as needed, scraping of the Adam's apple to hide its prominence, and even a tweaking of the vocal chords to raise the tone of the individual's voice.

In fact, I have seen (for research, I assure you) several ladyboys' lower bits. Once, it was in the company of my wife, who was a friend of the "unfinished" post-op "girl". I noted in almost all cases a slight "extra-labial" scarring, and the tell-tale lack of a clitoris. Although one "girl", who had gone through the process with a well-financed sponsor, proved different.

She assured me that the small bud hat was hidden under a clitoral hood. Although it was a fake medical construction, it added pleasure during sexual intercourse. Her doctor was good, the bits looked real, and the scarring was minimal, scarring which could easily be hidden by allowing even a minimal amount of pubic hair growth.

Indeed, the result of this transformation is a "woman" of significant beauty, who many of those unfamiliar with Thailand would not guess was anything but a stunning female beauty. In fact, Thai women, when asked about how to identify ladyboys, will often say you can spot a ladyboy because she is "too beautiful" or "too perfect". One natural and sufficiently attractive Thai female commented with a sulk, "I would be just as beautiful as a ladyboy if I could afford half the surgeries he's had."

Thai women, even when quite beautiful, loath their unpronounced depressed noses, and prefer the more pronounced bridges of most Western noses. Most Thai women would jump at the chance of rhinoplasty, or a "nose job".

Then, of course, there is always the breasts. Most women, even Western, wouldn't turn down the opportunity to have a breast augmentation, unless they are naturally blessed already. For Thai women, being naturally blessed is almost an anomaly. Considering that breast augmentation is one of the basic surgeries ladyboys undertake in their transformation process, one can see why natural females might be a little jealous at not having the opportunity for self-improvement. Given that Thai girls' breasts are usually smaller than those of Western women, I have rarely met a Thai girl who would turn down the chance to have her breasts enhanced, a procedure my wife is currently pushing for and that I view as a "gift that keeps on giving"; a good investment, in my opinion.

One thing that makes Thai women even more sexy is the fact that many never bother with fashion. They can wear a simple T-shirt and jeans, maybe a miniskirt, and still end up looking great. The average Thai woman is not conscious of designer brands. This is left to the hi-so (high society), stars, and ladyboys.

There is also the daily primping and preening, hairstyling, make-up, and attention to fashion that complete the package. Some salons cater almost exclusively to ladyboys, and are often run by older ladyboys, but most beauty salons are of mixed clientele, having just as many real women customers. The daily preparations of hair and make-up seem to require an average of several hours of work.

And this is where water-cannon-aided fun becomes the bane of a *katoey*'s existence.

During Songkran, it's impossible to walk the streets of Bangkok's red-light district without being drenched. Several of the clubs in Patpong are exclusively ladyboy go-go bars, the most prominent of which is King's Castle on the corner of Patpong Soi 1, the crossroad named Soi Crazy Horse that connects Sois 1 and 2.

King's Castle could be one of the top ladyboy go-go bars in Bangkok as all of the "women" are those who have gone through sexual-reassignment surgery—and thus able to have intercourse with customers, should it be desired. I always enjoy the fun of taking first-time visitors and friends to Thailand to the bar just for a beer or two, allowing the newbies to flirt, frolic, pinch, and squeeze before informing them that every woman in the bar is, in fact, a man. Only one visitor—granted, an old Asia hand but new to Thailand—was able to realize something was amiss by the time the first beer had arrived.

The location of the bar, however, proves to be quite unfortunate for the working "girls" during Songkran. Trying to leave the bar with their customers, they become, like everyone else, an instant target of the water-soaked celebrations. Much to their chagrin.

In fact, in such a situation it is not unusual for a ladyboy to become rather vocally abusive with the person who has targeted him—it is always a *farang* as Thais would never show such disrespect to their "sisters".

Indeed, even as the evening draws to a close and the bars shut down, a half-dozen or so ladyboys huddle a safe distance from the oft-drunken partygoers, looking for a chance of safe passage. Some will plead their way through with a respectful *wai* (respectful prayer-like gesture of the hands), making their way down the streets with their hair and make-up intact.

On one such occasion, as the party wound down, a huddle of ladyboys decided to make a run for it en masse and started down the street. Only a few drunken revelers remained, but as one *farang* raised his water gun and took aim at the approaching ladyboys, a young Thai woman stopped him, shouting, "Hey, they work hard to be beautiful!"

Indonesian model Tiara Lestar shakes things up

August 2005's Dutch *Penthouse* magazine featured thirteen photos of twenty-three-year-old Indonesian beauty Tiara Lestar (a.k.a Amara, Tiara Lestari). *Penthouse* says that in the Far East, she is considered an international supermodel; the Naomi Campbell of Asia.

Tiara's motto is "Shocking Asia". She goes all the way, posing nude, which in some Asian countries (like Indonesia) is still not allowed. She also walks the catwalks in fashion shows. It seems Tiara Lestar and her photographer, Adam Yurman, have now set about hitting international men's magazines. Following her appearance in the Dutch edition of *Penthouse,* she was also featured in the Spanish edition of *Playboy*. She has also previously been featured in the Thai edition of *Penthouse*.

Adam Yurman from *Pacific USA*, who did the photo shoot for both *Penthouse* and *Playboy,* recently spoke with *Asian Sirens*. Adam explains why there is a big difference between Tiara's photo shoots as Amara (for *Pacific Beauty*) and the more recent shoots for *Penthouse* and *Playboy*.

"Tiara and I have been working on developing her career for about one and a half years. The first shooting we did was somewhat casual, and we did not know if there was going to be anything coming out of it. We had a not-so-great make-up artist and we just shot in a normal fancy hotel. It was almost a test rather than a shooting. Those photos were good enough to make the pages of the Thai [edition of] *Penthouse* but they went no further." The best was yet to come, Adam explains.

"[The] Second shooting with Tiara was better and we had a nice beach location in Phuket, Thailand. You can see bits of this shooting in the Dutch *Penthouse* as they are at the beach. This was the precise location where the tsunami hit and the hotel's rooms on the ground floor facing the beach where we were shooting were wiped away along with any people sunning there. Nice shots, bad memory. We shot there about one month before the wave hit."

Adam was then contacted by his agent who said *Playboy* wanted to publish photos of Tiara, and that he had better shoot something good. "So off we went to Tiara's home in Jakarta, Indonesia, and then on to the mystical island of Bali. We went to the jungle and found waterfalls; lush green mountains and two of the best make-up and hairstylists money can buy. About this time, Tiara was gaining a lot of experience as a model and she was hitting a higher peak.

"The photos were the best of anything we had shot and it was good timing because we had a hot customer waiting for them. She made the cover of *Playboy* and the cover of my *Pacific USA* calendar which I will [release] next month, September, on my website when the boat gets in with my shipment of calendars. I will write extensively about Tiara at that time, but for now she is shooting constantly and has landed a major TV show in her native Jakarta, and is happy as can bath in the light of her new-found stardom."

Crashing Down, January 2006

Contrary to her motto of "Shocking Asia", Tiara turned out to be quite unhappy when her native Indonesia turned out to be especially shocked by her nude photos. Tiara appears to be unfamiliar with the Internet and how things—especially porn—have a way of getting around on it.

The pictures from the aforementioned photo shoots made their way onto the Internet, as they usually do, and then found their way to Indonesia. Seeing as Indonesia is the world's most populous Muslim nation, it is sufficient to say that people were not pleased.

So, as a matter of course, pictures were burned, *fatwah*s were issued, and the once-rising model and starlet found herself in a much more unwelcoming environment than she'd expected in her native homeland.

In a situation that just seems to add insult to injury, the Indonesian edition of *Playboy* was preparing to launch in January 2006, just as the Tiara Lestar scandal was in full fervor. Somehow the fact that Tiara had posed for *Playboy* made her a poster child (to be burned, of course), as the Muslim nation voiced its displeasure with the new men's magazine.

In January 2006 Tiara chose to speak out on her blog about her experiences.

"I respect *Playboy* as an internationally known publication. Everyone, from legendary Marilyn Monroe to Pamela Anderson to Madonna to Cindy Crawford have benefited from their professional relationships with the magazine.

"I made a personal decision as a model to also follow that route last year. This decision certainly wasn't popular in my own country. Heck, it was a huge disappointment for my parents too.

"I regret that part of it. For that, I am sorry. For my parents who I love very much and for them alone, I have made another personal decision to not pursue that line of work anymore. Being on the cover of *Playboy* can be considered [the] peak of any model's career. As they say, 'Been there done that.'

"However, I was aware of one thing; I appeared in a

country that does not consider Playboy and nudity as taboo. My appearance was never intended for consumption of Indonesia. How many Indonesians do you know read *Playboy* Spain? My pictures circulating on the Internet happened without my being consulted. I do not have rights to those pictures. Not offending my countrymen was one of the criteria of my decision-making process in appearing in *Playboy* Spain."

"Internet", Tiara, you know, "I-N-T-E-R-N-E-T". The global pornography network—sorry, information network—was Tiara's downfall. Her not understanding that the pictures would, of course, eventually make the Internet and thus know no borders seems to be a bit naive on her part, but she doesn't accept that: the pictures were meant for Europe, not Indonesia.

To this, bloggers on *Asian Sirens* stated that, "Tiara, as a 'cosmopolitan woman of the world', [should] have known that appearing in *Playboy* Spain (and *Penthouse* Holland and Thailand) would mean that these images could find their way to [the Internet and thus] Indonesia. This is the information age. Everything we say or do is captured somewhere on the web. Once a photo is out there, someone will scan it or rip it off a site and it will never go away and travel the world in a split second. [Surely she] must have realized this?"

Standing Up, June 2006

On her blog, Tiara Lestar says that she is no longer happy posing nude in men's magazines and would rather find an alternative way to make money. She has even asked her readers to participate in a poll to help her make up her mind.

The original versions of the poll's questions were in Bahasa Indonesian and that unfortunately excludes non-Indonesians from participating. That's why the *Indonesian Celebrities* site has set up its own version of her poll in English, with a couple of additional career options (and no, "porn star" was not an option).

Tiara, who was once a rising model, now faces ridicule all over the world, and especially in her native and conservative homeland of Indonesia where her career has sunk.

To appease her family, on April 1, 2006 she agreed to an arranged marriage. Tiara still models in a part-time and non-nude capacity. Based upon her earlier modeling work, one could conclude that her husband is a lucky fellow.

Compiled reporting, August 2005 to June 2006

Asian Sirens contributed to these reports.

China Barbie
takes on Mattel

Earlier this month, Mattel, which makes Barbie dolls, was forced to recall millions of toys that were made in China because of lead paint and loose magnets that presented dangers to consumers. So what's their next step in recovering from possible lost revenues? To attack the Asian-American porn star "China Barbie" of ChinaBarbie.com, of course.

Rather than focusing on its own legal problems and trying to make amends, the major US toy-making corporation has decided to take aim at suing the budding porn queen China Barbie for her comparatively nominal monetary assets. But why? Is it seriously for money that any barrister, paralegal, or law clerk worth their salt could have informed Mattel doesn't exist?

Okay, so there is no money to recover—then why? It seems that China Barbie is suddenly—after seven-plus years of porn production—putting the mainstream, conservative (long-legged, busty, ultimately beautiful) image of Barbie in jeopardy by associating her with hardcore pornography. It would seem that Mattel's Barbie dolls are under threat, at least in their opinion anyway.

"The site's been up for like five years, so it's like, why are they coming after me right now?" She is right to question the trademark-infringement lawsuit leveled at her website ChinaBarbie.com by the California-based toymaker.

"It's because they're in trouble right now with the lead poisoning thing, and everyone's been Googling it and that's how they found out about the site," she told Hasani Gittens of the *New York Post* in a recent interview.

"I'm not marketing myself to children, in any way shape or form," said China Barbie, whose real name is Terri Gibson. While she incorrectly notes, in legal terms, that she is not marketing to children as a point of the litigation, the fact remains that her marketing does not necessarily infringe Mattel's intellectual property (IP) rights.

Regardless of the outcome of this recent lawsuit, long-time fans of China Barbie are rallying around her, many through her website and her Adult Yahoo! Group. Some are offering simple donations to a "legal fund", while others are offering legal services, (which seem questionable). The most popular are offers from people to be her co-star so she can earn more money from pornography.

The tactic being undertaken by Mattel is especially questionable in this case. Often intellectual property owners who file lawsuits in similar circumstances can lose the case.

The United States Patent and Trademark Office (USPTO) and US Federal Courts generally opine that using a personal name to identify an individual does not give rise to infringement or damages unless the individual is seeking to identify with and purposefully use intellectual property of the complainant. Which China Barbie is not.

She would have to be using advertising and marketing materials, slogans, images, or other materials originally put out by Mattel. This would then confuse consumers, and cause unfair competition or brand identity dilution. China Barbie has done none of these things.

"Barbie" is a common name, but is also a trademark owned

by Mattel for certain commercial purposes, and has certain limitations. The word "Barbie" is trademarked in the US (and beyond) by Mattel. "China", of course, cannot be trademarked for a myriad of reasons but essentially that it is the name of a country and thus too generic.

However, the word "China Barbie" would, likely, be a valid registration—if it wasn't the current subject of objection. Many onlookers would bet that Mattel's intellectual property attorneys are working overtime to register "Barbie of China", "China Barbie", "Chinese Barbie", or similar word marks to arm themselves in this campaign. Therefore if someone was to try to register "China Barbie" now, they wouldn't have a prayer because Mattel's lawyers would contest it, or would have already filed it.

There is still the issue that China Barbie is using the name as a personal moniker, without seeking to use or infringe Mattel's IP rights. Any long-term court battle might end up ruling against Mattel, in China Barbie's favor.

Even the domain name that Mattel is fussing over—which is part of the lawsuit—does not enhance their claim. The Domain Name System (DNS) Registrar that allowed China Barbie to register and use ChinaBarbie.com stands strongly on a first come, first served basis. If Mattel want the site now, they would have to make her an offer she couldn't refuse.

Mattel had the opportunity to spend their millions long before China Barbie to buy up any domains they felt might represent a threat—either immediate or in the future—to their IP rights. That might sound ominous for owners of intellectual property, but it is not; if Miss Barbie had used the domain in question to somehow infringe on the IP rights of Mattel—in any manner noted above—they could contest it. However, usually the first step is making a complaint with the Uniform Domain-Name Dispute-Resolution Policy (UDRP), an arbitration board provided by Internet

Corporation for Assigned Names and Numbers (ICANN) before taking it to the US Federal Courts in a trademark claim.

In either case, for successful prosecution by the plaintiff, she would have to have used Mattel images, products, or advertising to promote her site and/or work, which she hasn't.

Unlike China Barbie, Mattel doesn't seem to have legs in this case. So why are they bothering to spend tens of thousands of dollars to prosecute?

It could be summarized by two words: "China" and "Barbie", probably also mixed with "production", "lead", "trade", "labor", "paint", "magnets", and "Mattel" versus what you might find by just searching for "China Barbie". For Mattel it would appear to a public relations campaign: while they are being lambasted in the West for producing in a trade pariah like China a product that might be dangerous because of lead or paint, Mattel's PR guru's can turn everyone's attention to this "slut, porn star" who is misusing their good, honorable name.

It's always true that sex news and scandal always draws the crowds. If you were Mattel, what would you rather have: Google News return hundreds of results about a "porn star using Barbie's good name"; or similar results for your corporation's failure to effectively manage quality control, product safety, and material sourcing in what has become a trade pariah in the eyes of US consumers? The answer seems quite clear, and their actions seem to only confirm this.

Often the methodology of larger businesses and corporations is to bleed their foes through litigation. Smaller organizations, like China Barbie, have nowhere near the resources to successfully fight an attack from a company like Mattel. The well-funded bullies (plaintiffs) can win simply by having the resources to fund a team of lawyers to file stacks of motions against the defendant—in this case China Barbie. Obviously can't even afford the legal team to answer the case, let alone argue it in open court. As a result, the courts will interpret this failure to answer the proceedings as acquiescence, and rule with a default judgment in favor of the plaintiff. A default win.

Mattel and their IP attorneys might realize that the validity of their claim against China Barbie is shaky at best, and certainly one that would recover damages, but it seems the job is not to recover assets. The aim is probably more to do with using disinformation and redirection for public relations reasons. Mattel may be playing the victim, but to those who understand the full situation in legal and media terms, Mattel is creating a victim for their corporate well-being.

The lady works alone—or does she?

The Suzie Wong days of Hong Kong may be something of an era long passed, but today's Hong Kong is no less the sexual temptress. From the hip central district of Lan Kwai Fong, to Wan Chai's bustling bar district, to Tsim Sha Tsui which caters more to local Chinese, the city is a diverse metropolis offering a range of adult pleasures and liaisons.

The most famous area is probably Wan Chai, which is where the Suzie Wong story originates. It is a red-light district with go-go bars, pubs, nightclubs, and "freelance" bars. Suffice to say that some of these bars are so jammed with women that the women outnumber male patrons 4–1. They come from all over the world. Most are from East and Southeast Asia, but one can easily chat up a Colombian, Russian, or Ukrainian girl on any given night.

Some are exclusively working the bars as freelancers; others work in Hong Kong's formidable healthcare/housekeeping industry, and take the occasional night out for fun and the chance to augment their income. These domestic helpers earn an average, paltry sum of HK$3,450 (US$500) a month. So it is easy to see why the bars are a draw for them, when on a single evening they can charge a customer as much as HK$1,000 (US$125) for a roll in the hay. Other women will tell you they are genuinely looking for a boyfriend or husband, possibly in all the wrong places.

Lan Kwai Fong is decidedly more upper class, and there are

no bars teeming with working girls there. For the most part, a guy may stumble across the occasional freelancer, usually Chinese—sometimes even locals and not mainlanders—but these local delights, like the district they are found in, prove to be top-shelf, charging a usual base of HK$2,000 (US$250) or much more.

Instead, most will find that this area is the "yuppie" party district where middle- to upper-class women, *gweilos* (foreigners) and locals alike come to relax, have a good time, and be seen in this trendy crowd. Here, a guy is more likely to find a nice Chinese girl looking for a proper relationship than a one-night stand.

Tsim Sha Tsui is notably more for the locals; it is dominated by Chinese bars for Chinese customers. To navigate them effectively a newcomer would do better to have a Chinese mate. In these bars a Westerner has to come to terms with lackluster English skills, strange delicacies (chilled chickens' feet?!), and the Chinese ways of entertainment. You do not just order a whiskey or a beer, but a bottle of Chivas or a twelve-pack of bottled beers, brought to the table in buckets of ice. Let us also not forget karaoke, for when you are in these bars it seems omnipresent.

The most popular places in this district for a guy seeking some companionship are probably the karaoke/hostess-style bars. These may be one large open bar or a whole building converted into private karaoke rooms, which are often plush and lavishly appointed. Invited by a Chinese friend during my early days in Hong Kong, I met him at such a venue, and found him sitting alone in an expansive and luxurious space that could probably hold twenty people comfortably.

A quick chat on the private room's phone and a waiter seemed to materialize seconds later. A bottle of whiskey, a bucket of beers, and some food that I could not identify were ordered, all in Cantonese, of course. With that, my friend turned from the waiter and asked me, "What do you think is good?" Apparently he had failed to realize that everything up to that point had been in Cantonese and I was generally lost. He realized his error and turned back to the waiter.

"*Lok, lok* (Six, six)," he said. That I understood, but I didn't know its context.

The plasma TV on the wall was randomly flipping through songs as a team of waiters and waitresses assembled glasses, ice, stirrers, soup, plates, silverware, chopsticks, napkins, beer, whiskey, and an array of food. And as quickly as they had come, they were gone again. Left alone, my friend mixed drinks while I ensured that what I believed to be sea creatures on a plate close to me were, in fact, dead.

Before I had a chance to ask, there was a knock at the door and it swung open. Six Chinese girls in see-through negligees, under which they were wearing only G-strings, poured into the room.

"*Hoa, hoa, lok* (Okay, okay, six)," I said, giving my friend a knowing wink.

The beautiful and nearly naked women sat down and cozied up to us, drinks were handed out to all, and the night began in earnest. Karaoke was soon being belted out, food disappeared—and was often replaced—in rapid succession. Karaoke, I found, is far more tolerable when you have a naked woman on either side of you. In fact, karaoke being sung to me sexily, even in a foreign language, by a naked woman borders on being likable.

This is sort of an "anything goes" environment and as the liquor flows, anything can happen. The girls set the boundaries but these seem to be rather permissive, as one can grope, squeeze, nibble, bite, pinch, suck, diddle, and plant kisses just about anywhere the imagination may lead. The girls are available for short-time companionship in yet another private room. This is negotiable with them and at their option; they are not required to go with a customer. They can also be taken out of the club completely for a night out on the town and more. Finally, I have it on good sources that impromptu orgies in these rooms are not necessarily unheard of. From the raunchy evening we had, I can well believe it. By the same token, this sort of entertainment is not for everyone, and certainly not for those on a budget. Four hours in a private room, including the hourly rates for the girls (billed like high-end attorneys at six-minute intervals), and enough food and alcohol for everyone ran a cool HK$7,000 (US$875); keep in mind, for that price we didn't even buy out any of the girls for sex.

There is yet another option for those seeking the company of a lady in Hong Kong. These are sometimes dubbed "one-girl apartments". Prostitution is technically legal in Hong Kong, but police criminalize it using Section 147 of the Crimes Ordinance, which makes it an offense to solicit for an immoral purpose. Brothels are illegal, possibly with the aim being to break up organized prostitution. But interestingly, a loophole seems to exist that allows a single woman in an apartment to act legally as a sex worker.

To a large extent, these girls are believed to be run by Hong Kong's organized crime syndicates, and this is probably true. During a recent visit to one such address, I noticed no fewer than six unfriendly looking gentlemen hanging around the small lobby near to the apartment of the girl I was visiting. Yes, she was available, I was told, and available for one hour at HK$600 (US$75).

It was probably at this same point that my hesitation caused a problem. Chatting up the triads is not recommended. The "leader" was a guy I mentally nicknamed "Flash" because of his trendy clothes and hairdo. His English was passable, and he was apparently not pleased that I didn't want to just plop down six hundred bucks and head in to do my business. Instead I began asking questions.

The guy seated behind him near the door to the apartment—whom I mentally noted should be called "Tiny" because of his stunning girth—furrowed his brow, and this was the first sign that things had gone awry. A question or two later, this time by Flash, and I found myself in the unwanted embrace of Tiny, while a couple of the four "foot soldiers" searched me. As an additional note: a business card that identifies you as a journalist is also not something to take into such an environment.

After I was told not to come back, Tiny deposited me in the elevator and I was on my way, marginally educated from the experience. I decided a different approach might be in order.

As usual, the Internet proved useful for my research as I soon found sites that listed, and even rated, these one-girl-apartment sex workers. Thousands of listings are online, and after spending far too long browsing, I decide on a girl named Pak Suet, billed as a half-Chinese, half-Japanese who, importantly, spoke English (along with Japanese and Cantonese). The site told me she was an "outcall" girl, though the site listed mostly one-girl-apartment girls ("incall"), but after my previous experience I decide that this was probably a good thing.

I dialed the number and got what I presumed to be a *mamasan*.

"Yes, yes, Pak Suet can come," she said. "Yes, she speak English very good. Good more me!" Her laugh seemed to turn to a choking cough. I made arrangements and the *mamasan* told me there was a short-time hotel that would meet our needs. The services were sold under the guise of a massage.

"You one hour, one hour half, two hour?" she asked. I decided an hour and a half should suffice.

"What you want? Massage hand, massage mouth, full

massage?" I told her "massage hand" would be fine, surmising that this was a massage with a hand job. I presumed that a "massage mouth" was massage with a blowjob, and a "full massage" was a massage with sex. I then began to wonder if the girl actually knew how to give a massage, but considering that a ninety-minute hand job would be especially painful, I was hopeful of her massage skills.

The day arrived and I honored my appointment, entering the short-time hotel and settling the bill for the room. I was showed to the room by a bellboy, if he could be called that, and found Pak had already arrived. She was sitting on an armchair beside the bed; the room was far better appointed than I had expected.

Pak was gorgeous, and I immediately decided that the pictures on the site did her no justice. The effect, though, was that I was standing frozen, without a clue what to do next.

Pak wore a silken robe and was flipping though a local magazine. She immediately turned her attention to me, tossing the magazine on to the night table nearby. She looked over the awestruck *gweilo* for a moment, and finally got up and approached me.

"You speak English, yes?" she asked me warmly with a smile.

"Um, yeah," I blushed as I found myself attempting to retreat behind the tiny fire-escape plaque hung on the back of the door. When she reached me, she wrapped her hands around my hips.

"It's okay, relax," she cooed, and kissed me on the cheek. "Just you, me, stay together, massage, what you want, okay?"

I whimpered something along the lines of "okay" and she smiled and backed off. She conducted a brief moment of business and relieved me of HK$800 (US$100).

"Take off your clothes!" she directed.

I shifted my weight nervously and wiped a bit of unexpected

sweat from my brow—the room was air conditioned, mind you. I hesitated. Maybe I should just take off my shirt to appease her?

She turned away from me and walked a few paces to the night stand, where she lit some incense and deposited the bounty in her purse. She faced me again and dropped her robe to the floor. She was now completely naked a few feet away from me. She was stunning and uninhibited. Understandably so: she was a beautiful specimen, if ever there was one.

"We take shower, off clothes!" she demanded.

I was no longer in complete control and stripped without compunction. She started the shower and I entered the bathroom tentatively. She scolded my behavior.

"You have problem? I'm not beautiful? You not want?" she asked with scorn, despite already knowing most of the answers; any man who didn't want her could probably be deemed a homosexual.

"I'm married," I sputtered as she stepped into the shower.

She looked at me with fleeting disdain and replied, "So are most men I have for customer. Come, take shower!"

I dropped my boxers and decided a shower was in order to cleanse myself, besides, the target of my story demanded it, right?

She washed every bit of my body, lathering me up with soap, and even stroking certain bits to excitement that edged on climactic. I stopped her and said, "No, massage is okay." She smiled.

"Okay, wash me!" she directed, handing me the bar of soap. I groaned in lust. Was she serious? She was, and I rubbed the bar of soap over her breasts, the small of her back, and her buttocks.

"You need wash pussy," she said, pushing the bar of soap in my hand to her groin. I submitted to the moment as Pak kissed me tenderly.

A laugh escaped her and she seemed to keep me at a distance as her body heaved in pleasure as I stroked her. "Alright, finish shower!" she declared, pushing my hand away finally with a smile. "You out!"

I obeyed, overly stimulated, and headed out to the bedside seat. I had a problem that I was far too aroused to hide.

"Lie down!" she said, and without any protest I did. She was, of course, still naked and I had a strong desire to experience this visually, but I found myself lying on my stomach with her sitting on my lower back.

She was on top of me, massaging me. Her hands rubbed, cajoled, and loosened the muscles in my back. Meanwhile, I had a hard time ignoring her groin grinding on my tailbone. At some point I was unsure whether she was massaging me for my pleasure or her own because she seemed to be masturbating herself on my body. All in all, I decided that this was a nice distraction.

"Turn over!" she finally demanded.

"Um, I like this, I am okay," I responded.

"Need massage front! Turn over!" she instructed.

I groaned and turned over. The biggest problem I had was that despite extensive effort I was at full attention. Hiding my stimulation was not an option, and she gave a few cursory strokes of my erection. A hand job certainly seemed an acceptable outlet at this point.

"Massage," I beckoned, and suddenly and surprisingly she backed off. She massaged my chest, biceps, arms, even my hands, all the while stroking on, over or near my erection.

She slithered up my body, giving me more of an erotic experience than a massage. Suddenly, she shifted to a sort of "reverse cowgirl" position. Putting her groin about a foot from my face, she massaged my hips, then my thighs, moving down my body to my calves and feet while grinding herself against me all the way. The sensation was quite titillating, to say the least.

All too soon this too came to an end. I estimated I had been there for about an hour at this point while this naked beauty writhed over my body. Finishing off on the feet, she repositioned herself again, this time between the legs, and went in for the kill, offering a hand job, which I refused.

"Massage okay, very good!" I said truthfully.

With this she ran her nails lightly and playfully over me in a tickle that sent chills up my spine.

"You pay for hand job? You want blowjob? Sex?" she seemed to plead. She was seemingly anxious to please.

"No, no, no problem. I only want massage, and you give very good massage, thank you," I said, untangling myself, finding my pants and presenting her with another HK$100 (US$12.50) as a tip. This seemed to convince her that I was "satisfied".

We chatted for a few minutes as we composed ourselves and she made me promise to call her again soon. During this chat I tried to glean a few facts such as to whether she worked for anybody else. She said she didn't. More questions and she became a bit agitated by the interest, so I dropped it. I promised to call again soon. She pecked my cheek as I left the room.

Stepping out into the midday sun and lighting a cigarette, I considered the website and answering service that had helped to make this encounter possible, and doubted that she could truly be working alone. Looking around, I saw Hong Kong bustling as usual, people walking hurriedly, some queuing for food at a nearby shop, but one guy caught my attention. About a half-block away, a young guy dressed more for an evening out than a day of business seemed to linger around but, more importantly, even from behind his sunglasses he seemed to glance at me once or twice.

I began walking in the opposite direction, turning toward a

footbridge that lead to a nearby subway station before deciding to cut back to cross the street again, blending into the thick afternoon crowds. Finding a vantage point, I saw my man on the street was finishing a phone call. Minutes later, Pak Suet emerged from the hotel in a cute little summer dress and walked directly to a black BMW. As the guy got in the driver's seat, she hopped into the passenger seat, and soon they disappeared in the Hong Kong traffic.

Who really knows? He could be a bodyguard of some sort to ensure the girl's safety from stalkers or other abuse. However, when analyzing the Hong Kong sex and entertainment industry, more often than not one will find a large and organized syndicate facilitating the trade.

This guy was more likely to be her triad handler.

Japan's Lolita merchants feel the heat

Japan was slow in updating its child pornography laws to bring them into line with those of the West. It was only in 1999 and 2003 that Japan caught up, with the passage of new laws that made it illegal to produce, distribute, sell, possess, or trade in child pornography. Before 1999, it was only illegal to produce it.

Yet enforcement of the new laws has been lax, although that may have changed in the past month.

Fans and producers of a lucrative fad called "lolicon" got a wake-up call with the arrest of a publisher last month. Lolicon is a slang portmanteau of the phrase "Lolita complex", or "Lolita icon". The industry produces photo books and magazines with teenage and pre-teen models, sometimes as young as eight years old. The format is usually "near nudity" or "implied nudity", but a recent photo set featuring a fourteen-year-old girl went too far.

"The girl's swimsuit was deliberately made to be see-through. It was so tight-fitting you could make out the shape of her genitalia, and she'd been posed in such risqué positions that the Metropolitan Police Department decided to arrest the maker for breaking the law banning child pornography, even though the girl hadn't actually exposed her bust or between her legs," a reporter told *Weekly Playboy*.

The arrest was the first of its kind in Japan, where child pornography laws were enforced in a case where the model was not actually nude.

In a similar case in Hong Kong last year, the editor of *Easy Finder* Yuen Choi-yuk was ultimately cleared of child pornography charges after the magazine featured pictures of the then fourteen-year-old pop singer and model Renee Lee Wan wearing a semi-transparent white dress soaked in water. Although cleared of the charge, the editor was admonished for his lack of judgment.

Leung Tin-wai, the head of the journalism department at Hong Kong's Shue Yan College, warned that better judgment must be used in editorial and decision-making processes. He also questioned why it was that the magazine saw fit to publish such wet-T-shirt-style photos in an effort to convey the sex appeal of a fourteen-year-old girl.

This new case in Japan concerning the recent indecent photo set is proving similar in many ways. If convicted, the publisher could face a maximum of three years in jail and a fine of 100,000 yen (US$930).

Up until this arrest, the lolicon industry had been quite lucrative for the Japanese publishing community. *The Japan Times* reported that "over three million of the photo books were sold in 2006–2007".

"Ever since the arrest, makers of products featuring teens in erotic poses have been in a state of panic. If material is judged to be overly obscene, people can be arrested for breaking the Child Pornography Law, even if the model is dressed in a swimsuit," an employee of a medium-sized DVD manufacturer producing material featuring models under fifteen years old told *Weekly Playboy*. "DVD shops and wholesalers are now on their guard, and have stopped taking materials featuring models under fifteen, even if the product looks like being a surefire seller."

It remains unclear why just the under-fifteen section of the industry, sometimes referred to as U15, is being affected as child prostitution and pornography laws clearly define "child" as a person under the age of eighteen. Yet the industry continues to use girls aged sixteen and seventeen years old.

The manga (Japanese for "print cartoons and comics") industry also remains unaffected by the new crackdown. Pornographic drawings and cartoons that depict children remain legal—and lucrative.

Figures for the total value of the Japanese child pornography industry are hard to come by, but annual sales of manga alone in 2000 amounted to over 600 billion yen (US$5.5 billion), nearly one quarter of the total sales of all published material. It is estimated that 30–40% of manga contains sexual themes or content, much of it representing schoolgirls of elementary or junior high school age wearing uniforms. Themes include rape, sado-masochism, *bukkake* (where multiple men ejaculate on a female's face), and bondage. About half of the 2,000 pornographic animation titles distributed in Japan every year, including films and video games, feature schoolgirl characters.

Lolicon manga are usually short stories published in media specializing in the genre, and are bought predominantly by white-collar men in their twenties and thirties. A common focus of these stories is taboo relationships, such as between a teacher and student, or a brother and sister. Sexual experimentation between children is another popular theme.

Last October, the Japanese government issued the results of its Special Opinion Poll on Harmful Materials, in which 86.5% of respondents said that manga and art should be subject to regulation for child pornography, while 90.9% said that "harmful materials" on the Internet should be regulated. The current child pornography laws in Japan do not regulate manga and art that depict children who are not real, or "virtual child pornography".

As Japan struggles to reign in various forms of child

pornography to reach compliance with the views of the international community, largely influenced by the far more conservative Western societies of Europe and North America, there will ultimately be a reckoning in the publishing industry for it to get in line with these new standards. It is a reckoning that is bound to cost the industry hundreds of millions of dollars in sales. Yet it remains to be seen if Japanese authorities will move beyond token enforcement and adopt a more hard-line stance, which would be the real turning point in the prolific trade of child pornography in Japan.

First published February 23, 2008 in *Asia Times Online*

My big fat triad wedding

Triads are strange bedfellows that one can find oneself among in Asia's sex industry. Hong Kong is, of course, no exception, as the various aspects of its sex industry seem under the influence, at varying levels, of these Chinese organized crime syndicates.

I guess I shouldn't have been so surprised, then, when I found a story where I certainly wasn't looking for one. Most evenings after finishing work, I would make my way to a bar in the nearby Wan Chai district, better known as Hong Kong's primary red-light district, for a quiet drink. At that hour the bar was always nearly empty.

After just a few hours it would be teeming with hundreds of girls—mostly from Thailand, but some from the Philippines—and *gweilo*s drinking with the girls working the sex trade on a freelance basis, as well as men seeking female companionship. But in the early evenings there were only a few girls and a couple of older Chinese regulars; the music was set to a low din and I could have a drink and usually read in peace.

It was a bar that reminded me of ones in Thailand, since most of the girls were from there, and I could practice my Thai and generally impress the girls by speaking their language—and alleviate some of my homesickness at the same time. But mostly I just went there early to read, have a drink or two, and then head home.

That was exactly what I was planning one evening when a cute little Korean girl—a consummate professional and always looking for an early score—came bouncing over and tried to get friendly.

Sensing that I didn't want to chat too much, she took another approach. "So what are you reading?" she asked, tentatively reaching over to see the book's cover. "*Dragon Syndicates*. Oh, pictures." She took the book and began flipping through the pages, which contained different gangster photos—not Al Capone-type stuff but relating to the triads, symbols, high-ranking historical figures, etc. She stopped at a photo of a known triad temple somewhere in Hong Kong.

"I think I know this temple! I don't think it is far from here," she said, then asked: "Do you know where this is?" She showed me the page in the book.

The caption didn't list the district. "I don't know," I replied. "It doesn't say."

With this she slumped a bit, murmured something that sounded Korean, and then looked up at the Chinese bartender and asked him if he knew where the temple was, holding out the book to him.

"Um," I said, caught off guard, raising my hand fruitlessly to stop her.

The bartender took the book, studied the photo for a second, and then looked up at her and then at me. He thumbed a few pages back in the photo section, then a few pages forward. Without a word, he went to the other side of the bar and put the book in front of the largest Chinese fellow sitting there. "Uh-oh," I said to myself. The Korean girl looked at me quizzically.

The Chinese guy picked up the book and also began flipping through the pages. Finally he asked the bartender a question. The bartender said something, and then slightly nodded in my direction. The old Chinese guy glanced up, briefly meeting my eyes, then looked back down at the book. He said something to the bartender, who nodded and walked off. The Chinese man stood, walked around the bar, and slammed the book down in front of me, still open to the page with the temple photo.

"You want to know about this temple?" he asked somewhat forcefully. I said nothing. "It is in Sheung Wan. I don't know why a man would want to come into a bar like this, with beautiful women"—he indicated the Korean who now sat frozen next to me—"and read trash like this. Don't bring this back here again." He stalked back to his seat, glared at me once more and returned to conversing with his friends.

After an awkward, shell-shocked silence, the Korean girl sheepishly apologized.

"No, don't worry about it," I said. "I should have known better than to bring this book here, but I didn't really think about it."

"I am sorry anyway," she said, then excused herself. "I am going to go say hello to a friend."

I ordered another drink, trying to be nonchalant about what had just happened, but did not dare to resume reading the book. After finishing and paying for my drink, I made for the exit, but was caught just before the door—by the Korean girl.

"Here is my phone number," she said, handing me a folded napkin. "I am in town for about a month. Give me a call—maybe we can get a drink or something." With that, she turned and went back to join her friends and I made my exit.

You might think this episode would have put me off this bar, but I am not easily deterred and, as I said, I liked the place. Over the following weeks I continued to go back and read, though of course not *Dragon Syndicates* (which is quite a good book, by the way). On one such evening, I looked up from my book and saw the old Chinese guy playfully furrow his brow as he straightened up and looked questioningly at the book I was reading. I lifted it to show him the cover. He smiled, nodded, and lifted his glass in a toast, which I reciprocated.

Strangely, in the coming weeks a sort of standoffish camaraderie grew between us. Salvos of drinks would be sent back and forth across the bar. Though I hadn't noticed before, he was obviously the top guy among the Chinese. Not only was he larger and took charge, but while the other Chinese men talked over the top of each other in typical Chinese fashion, the moment he spoke they listened attentively, not daring to interrupt.

Thus the bar became an even more intriguing and enjoyable hangout for me. Add to this the fact that I had grown keen on a cute Filipina bartender there, and you could definitely say it was my favorite haunt. The Filipina was a full-breasted number, thin, not particularly tall, but with a nice pert, upturned bum that I swear you could balance a bar glass on. She had long, luxurious hair that reached her tailbone.

The fact that I was now chatting up one of the bartenders was not lost on the Chinese guy. One night when I came later than usual, without a book in hand, to visit and flirt with the Filipina—named Rowena—the Chinese guy finally decided to come over and chat with me. We talked about work (I told him I was a computer guy, as I past experience had taught me that triad members are not very enthusiastic about journalists), Hong Kong, and similar banter, and I learned finally that his name was Fong.

"So are you the bar owner, or one of the managers?" I asked, having noted that he never paid for drinks.

"Oh no, I don't work for the bar at all," Fong said. "I supply the bar with what it needs."

"Like a liquor distributor?" I asked, already knowing this was wrong.

He looked at me, wryly sizing me up, and then said, "No, I supply this bar with a commodity far more important than alcohol. The girls, most of the girls, are mine." He swept his hand across the bar with a triumphant grin.

"That's got to be good business," I said simply.

"It is. Speaking of which, I noticed you seem to have taken a liking to Rowena," he said. I nodded in agreement.

"You know, it is a lot less hassle getting action on this side of the bar."

"Maybe I like the challenge," I said with a smile.

Fong smiled back. "I thought you would say something like that. Well, what with your books and chasing the bar staff, you seem determined to make sure I don't earn a dollar from you through my girls."

"You never know, maybe next time," I said.

He shook my hand. "Yes, maybe next time. Best you don't let Rowena hear that." And with that he moved off into the now-crowded bar to assume his regular seat among friends.

The Night Off

Rowena, who was twenty-six, and I had been out a few times and grown increasingly intimate, but on one of her nights off I was especially pleased when she showed up for our dinner date carrying a small bag. When I inquired about it, she described as an "overnight bag" with a wink and a frisky smile.

After a nice dinner, she asked me to come to another bar to meet one of her friends who worked there and have a few drinks. I happily agreed. We entered another bar in Wan Chai, not dissimilar to hers. We found her friend bartending, took a seat at the bar, and ordered drinks. As her friend was serving us I couldn't help noticing that she had the same tribal-style tattoo on her right wrist that I had noticed on Rowena.

After the girls had finished chatting in Tagalog and her friend had sized me up sufficiently, her friend went off to serve more drinks and we were left alone again. I asked, "So what does the tattoo mean? Your friend has the same one."

Rowena considered this for a moment—maybe she was thinking of lying—but finally replied, "It is a gang tattoo. I was in the Foreign Triad when I was young."

Dear God, what have I gotten myself into? I thought.

She gave up waiting for a response and continued: "It is nothing, really. I was young, it was stupid. Just petty stuff."

"You were in the triads? You are triad?" I asked, notably stunned. "What type of 'petty stuff'?"

"Not in 'the triads', the Foreign Triad. Only Chinese can be in the actual triads," she explained, then continued: "But they bring in foreigners to do petty stuff, making up the Foreign Triad. You know, running drugs, numbers, shakedowns, the prostitution rings ..."

"What? Prostitution rings?" I needed a drink, and signaled her friend as such.

"Hey, I was never in the sex industry. I had my son at eighteen, I told you that. I was a young mother and never would have gotten involved as a sex worker," she said defensively. "You know, they need help with the new girls, getting them settled, explaining the rules, daily rates for their rooms and food—it helps having someone who speaks their native language to do that. Then, of course, somebody has to collect the money every day."

To say I was stunned would be an understatement of epic proportions. But over the following months, through similar conversations and pillow talk, I came to learn from Rowena the ins and outs of the triad-run sex scene in Wan Chai and beyond.

The girls who work the Hong Kong bars are recruited for the triads back in their home countries by bargirls who have done the trip already, or by *mamasan*s connected to the triads as recruiters. These recruiters get a finder's fee and a commission from the new girl's income. Most of the new girls have to buy their own plane tickets, but a girl viewed as especially beautiful or having high potential might have the ticket bought for her, though she will have to pay it back through her work. Visas are arranged by the triad group from connections with the immigration police, who look the other way when the girls arrive and allow them entry; usually such a female traveling alone would be highly scrutinized on arrival in Hong Kong.

For example, when my Thai wife arrived in Hong Kong for the first time, she was pulled aside, detained, and questioned extensively until she provided a letter from me to the immigration police with a copy of my Hong Kong ID. After waiting more than an hour watching other travelers with the tell-tale BKK–HKG luggage tags diminish in the arrival lounge, I knew something was wrong. A call from the immigration police on my mobile finally came through. To say I was livid would be a pleasant understatement. I threatened to write a story for a prominent Hong Kong newspaper (I flashed my business card) that I worked for when I heard my wife sobbing in the background about immigration practices. An apologetic immigration officer showed up minutes later with my wife and her luggage, begging understanding.

The same thing happened thirty days later when I thought a nice weekend in Macau would be a good way to extend her visa for another month. Instead we found ourselves in an interrogation room upon our return to Hong Kong; me on suspicion of human trafficking, and her on suspicion of traveling for sex work. The Hong Kong department does not recognize Thai wedding certificates.

Such strict enforcement certainly begs the question: how can hundreds—no, thousands—of working girls be given a free pass on entry to Hong Kong, whereas those who are "not connected" are scrutinized extensively?

Once the working girls arrive, they are housed in apartments provided and run by the triad group. The room is usually a studio apartment with an offset bathroom. There are usually four to a room, sleeping in bunk beds or two double beds, a privilege for which they pay an average of HK$50 (US$7) a day. For this amount they are also provided with breakfast and lunch, or more like late lunch, early dinner, considering the hours they keep. Each meal is a simple small ration of rice and vegetables or meat. The girls are expected to fend for themselves for their late evening meal. They are assigned to a bar, and discouraged from going to others, except occasionally to ones run by the same triad group (unless they are in the company of a customer who it is assumed chooses the next establishment).

The money the girls earn comes from drinks that they get customers to buy for them, usually for the highly inflated average price of HK$130 (US$17), of which the girls get HK$20 (US$2.50), either paid on the spot or via a tiny slip or paper that they can to redeem for cash later. The bar obviously makes a huge profit on the overpriced drinks, and the girls are strongly encouraged to push lady drinks.

Of course the girls also make money from sex work. There are no barfines at these freelance places so the entire negotiated fee goes to the girl. The average price is about HK$1,500 (US$200), but can range from HK$1,000 (US$130) to HK$2,500 (US$320) for a girl who is a stunner or an opportunist. This fee is hers to keep, and a hard-working girl can earn several thousand US dollars a month; the idea is that the girl will have money for her family and herself and enough to buy another ticket to come back to her lucrative work after a trip home. Remember also that a girl returning home seemingly successful is a recruiting tool for her triad handlers, which perpetuates human trafficking for the sex trade and keeps the industry supplied with new girls. Of course, any girl going home will also been told about the finder's fee and commission in great detail before she leaves.

While, as noted above, the fee paid by a client for sex is the girl's to keep, it would be inaccurate to say that the syndicate gets nothing out of that part of the action. The girls usually pressure their clients into going to certain short-time hotels within walking distance of the bars, unless the customer has a hotel already or is a resident and wants to take them home, which is rare for a myriad of reasons. And who owns and operates the short-time hotels the girls direct their clients to? You guessed it: the triad group running the girls. At an average rate of HK$230 (US$30) an hour in hotels averaging twelve rooms each, with rooms turning over clients six to eight times a night, you can do the math and see the take is substantial. (For those who don't want to do the math, twelve rooms turning over seven times a night at HK$230 is HK$19,320, or about US$2,480, per location, per day.)

The triads pervade every element of bar life in Wan Chai; if a girl is addicted to drugs, the triad supplies it. Want to go home? Or better yet, maybe you want to work another month to make more money? Then the triads have the travel agent for you—not to mention a place to stay (and work) in mainland China or Macau while you await a re-entry visa to Hong Kong, Japan, Singapore, or Taiwan. They will take care of visas and immigration too, of course—for a fee. The doormen, bartenders, drug dealers, collectors, enforcers, drivers, handlers, runners, *mamasan*s when applicable, and, yes, bar owners are all connected at some level.

In this way girls can end up entering "The Circuit", sometimes chased by debt, addiction, or simply the desire to earn more money. The triads will offer Macau and mainland ports of call, not to mention trading girls off with the Japanese Yakuza to work as hostesses or straight-out prostitutes. Then they are sent on to Singapore, sometimes Taiwan, only to be brought back to Hong Kong—the Yakuza pays a commission to the triads in such cases, and vice versa. Fair trade, as they say. Welcome to The Circuit.

"How do you think I got my job?" Rowena asked me one night. "Competition is overwhelming for those jobs. If you think any one of those bartenders, managers, or doormen—Chinese and foreign alike (mostly Filipinos)—aren't connected, you're dead wrong." At least the Chinese had a promotional value and ability that she and foreign brothers and sisters did not. Still, she was thankful to have her job.

An Invitation You Can't Refuse

Weeks, maybe months, after "Rolie" (Rowena) and I had started our tryst, I was sitting in the bar far later than usual, though this had become more frequent. Now that we were sexually involved, Rolie had become possessive, and viewed any approaching female—especially Thais, with whom I share a language, much to her frustration—with deep animosity. To Rolie's dubious credit, she had a highly effective glare that said "move on or die" to any girl who dared chatting with me. She was not shy about showing her affection to mark her territory, which I found acceptable.

Mr Fong had also noticed the transition in our relationship. One night when Rolie was enjoying her fifteen-minute break with me in the nearly deserted VIP area, he approached her and asked that she follow him for a chat.

She immediately looked concerned, scared even. She turned and walked after him, glancing back in a way that made me worry even more. Minutes went by, but it felt like hours. I ordered a drink from a Filipina server who by this time I knew like a sister. She too seemed concerned by Rolie's absence, knowing full well with whom she was holding court.

When she reappeared, I said, "Rolie, your break is over. Do you have time? I don't want to get you in trouble." She'd get another break in an hour or so anyway.

She was dumbfounded, in every sense. "What did you say to him?" she asked, referring to Fong.

"Nothing! I didn't say anything!" I sputtered. "Why?" I feared for her job; she had a kid to look after.

But it was nothing like that. She lightened up and said, "I have been given an extra night off, paid, to attend a manager's wedding reception. Mr Fong told me to bring you. What did you do?"

"I didn't do anything. I only talked to him a few times," I said.

"Well, you made an impression," she replied with sincerity.

The Event

Rolie had told me time and again that I didn't need to buy a present, and thus scowled disapprovingly when she met me at the bar and saw the gift-wrapped box sitting in front of me: a Dolce & Gabbana wallet for the groom.

We walked a few blocks to a nondescript Hong Kong high-rise and took the elevator to the fourth floor. When the doors opened, the noise was overwhelming, like I'd stepped into a different world. Mahjong was being played, shots were had, pictures were taken, and people were chatting animatedly. I tried to take it all in as we entered, but it hit me all at once.

Sweet Jesus, I thought to myself, and then whispered to Rolie, "This is a triad wedding?!"

"Of course, what did you expect?" she replied quietly, taking my hand and leading me toward a table of her co-workers whom I now knew.

Pleasantries were exchanged, drinks were presented, and we

settled in at one of the "foreign" tables. I was amazed by how triad markings seemed to be everywhere. The congratulatory signs had well-known Chinese triad symbols written on them. Even when I glanced at people taking a group photo I caught one member of the group flashing a tell-tale hand gesture discreetly.

Ritual shots were taken of some Chinese moonshine that I'm sure enabled me to see through time. The happy couple came over to thank us for coming, and I offered my present to the groom, who was quite surprised. Rolie had been right: I think I was the only person who gave him a gift.

I was proved wrong, however, as later in evening a series of speeches kicked off. The groom was first, and from what I could gather he was mainly thanking guests for coming. His new bride was next, but the beautiful and demure young woman concluded after only a few short sentences. These were met with polite applause and calls of well-wishing and good luck.

Then there were a couple of family members who gave equally short speeches, and an older gentleman who seemed so close to tears that I figured he had to be the father of the bride.

Then the real speeches began. The first was from the female proprietor of the bar whom I had come to recognize after Rolie pointed her out a while before. Her speech drew bouts applause throughout, and she even switched to English at one point. She thanked the staff who were able attend for coming, drawing whoops of approval from our table and others. Then she seemed to get down to business, once again in Chinese so I was lost. The crowd was silent, listening attentively; I couldn't even ask Rolie (who spoke decent Cantonese) for subtitles. It was only when the bar owner dropped a bombshell as she concluded her speech that the crowd erupted in deafening applause. Some people stood and toasted with shouts of "*Yum tsaw*", and Rolie quickly explained that the owner had just officially announced the groom's promotion at the bar.

He would no longer work the bar in a polo shirt bearing the bar's logo and schlepping drinks as a bartender, but would now enter the ranks of management. In the coming months I would see him wearing finely pressed long-sleeved white dress shirts, pairs of smart pants, and even once appreciatively wielding in my direction the wallet I had given him with a proud nod and a thankful smile.

The best was yet to come it seemed, because after the revelry had calmed down, Mr Fong stepped up and took the microphone. The room fell silent as people took notice.

His speech was met with respect similar to that of the female owner's, but where she had drawn raucous applause at various moments, Fong instead drew practiced murmurs and incantations from the crowd. Even my table joined in but mainly it was from the mahjong corner, not to mention the "senior tables" placed near the front, close to the bride and groom.

Fong seemed in his element. He was a preacher speaking the gospel at that point and the clergy responded. In what I can only guess and piece together from Rolie's later descriptions, people answered with the equivalent of "preach the word, may success be upon us, we support those who believe [as we do]" or "in the words of the elders". Mr Fong's speech also turned in its climax to the idea of promotion, apparently. The more ritual responses did not cease, but the crowd became more boisterous and the joyous groom turned an ever-deeper shade of red. "He will have new responsibilities in his position," Rolie would later translate for me. "He was promoted, and he was promoted you understand?" I did understand. I had just witnessed a "49" being promoted to a "red pole" of the triad group. This is similar to a member of the Italian mafia going from the member of a "crew" to "captain" of his own crew, although there are sub-designations for each mafia family and syndicate that make these transitions and actual levels in the hierarchy unique and complex.

At one point in the evening, Mr Fong came by our table, shook my hand, and asked if we were enjoying ourselves. I said we were, adding that I was amazed.

"Yes, I thought you would enjoy it," he said with a smile and surveying glance around the room. He then excused himself and walked off to the mahjong corner. An eight-course dinner was served and we all ate, drank, laughed, and partied.

So there I was, an adopted member of one very unusual family. I appreciate that they took me into their circle and I was given a unique insight into a world that not many ever get to see.

But alas I will miss them, their revelry, camaraderie, and the experience they gave me. Because since you're reading this, you can imagine that it is not a family I plan on seeing any time again soon.

First published April 12, 2008 in *Asia Times Online*

When freaky-deaky
equals hara-kiri

In 2005, the Japanese population is believed to have peaked at about 127.5 million. Since then the figure has declined, with some estimates suggesting the population could shrink to 105 million by 2050. It's feared the drop will have a negative impact on the nation's labor force as well as grave social and economic consequences. Recent reports seem to indicate that the sexual proclivities of Japanese men are contributing adversely to the situation.

More and more men, reports maintain, are turning to masturbation sex toys and prostitution rather than to their female counterparts as wives or girlfriends. And further exacerbating an already declining birth rate of 1.29 children per women, found in a 2004 survey by *The Daily Yomiuri*, is the fact that some men are increasingly turning their backs on sex altogether.

"Sex is just way too much trouble," a thirty-five-year-old Japanese man told *Shukan Asahi* this week, adding that ever since he started using masturbation as a teenager, he's never desired a woman. "As long as I have a sex toy available, I don't need women. I can't come when I have sex, and you've got to put a lot of emotion into dealing with women. Self-pleasure is a hell of a lot less demanding than trying to please somebody else."

Pornography, masturbation aids, Internet porn sites, and social networks that lead to "virtual relationships", soaplands, and Japan's widespread prostitution industry all allow men outlets for sexual fulfillment while not fulfilling other needs, such as procreation. The alarming trend has led medical experts in Japan to coin a new term for a condition they call "vaginal ejaculation dysfunctional disorder".

"There has been a definite increase in the number of men showing signs of vaginal ejaculation dysfunction disorder, which includes such afflictions as premature and delayed ejaculation. There are physical reasons believed to be behind this, including prejudice against women, past trauma, and overuse of masturbatory aids so that a vagina is unable to provide sufficient stimulation," Dr Tsuneo Akaeda, head of the Akaeda Clinic in Tokyo's Roppongi entertainment district, told *Shukan Asahi*.

"Some of the masturbation aids coming out nowadays are absolutely incredible. Guys become used to using these and there is no doubt that many men are unable to obtain the necessary satisfaction from a female vagina that they need to ejaculate."

Meanwhile, Japan is quickly becoming the world's oldest population. By 2025, 27.3%, or 33.2 million people, will be aged over sixty, a study titled "The Illusion of Immigration Control" found.

Low birth rates coupled with the aforementioned sexual dysfunctions makes the problems that Japan faces immediate and daunting.

"With Japan's labor force expected to decrease by 10% in the next twenty-five years, the economic outlook is far from bright. In all likelihood, the domestic market will shrink, production will fall, the government's revenue base will contract inexorably, and it will struggle to meet welfare and medical payments for an increasing number of elderly as the dependency ratio (the number of workers supporting the elderly) will shift dramatically. In 1950, one elderly person was supported by twelve members of the working population, by 1990 it was 5.5 workers, and by 2020 it is estimated to be 2.3 workers. Naturally, the government is concerned about such a scenario," Julian Chapple wrote in a 2005 study titled "The Dilemma Posed by Japan's Population Decline".

The government has put forward a number of proposals to reverse the trend. These have included "Plus 1" (indicating the increase the government hopes to see to the birth rate), softening of immigration laws, child care initiatives, subsidies to parents for medical care and childcare, and working with Japanese employers to allow more flexi-time for parents. While the government has given the situation the appropriate attention, so far most of the initiatives have made little change and failed to stem the decline.

Japan, like many societies, can at times struggle with open communication and education about sex. So perhaps the answer is being overlooked: encourage more sex between partners and husbands and wives through better communication and education. Romance seems to have died in most forms in Japan, especially for married couples. A report by *Mainichi* cited that some 24% of married couples were sexless.

Reviving romance and passion among couples could be a solution to the problem. In a society that today relies on short-time courtesans, hostesses, geisha, soapland massage girls, and numerous other forms of prostitution for entertaining men in often sexless, or at least non-productive, sexual relations as far as procreation, one need only look to the Japanese response to Valentine's Day. The romantic holiday is a boom time for Japanese retailers, restaurants, love hotels, resorts, and intimate apparel distributors. Encourage more of these promotions year round; maybe even create a few Japanese specific Edo holidays.

In fact, encouraging romance and passion based upon the country's early sexual revolution during the Edo period of the seventeenth to nineteenth centuries could be the perfect recipe. By embracing and celebrating the Children of Edo—where sex was liberal, passionate, and openly discussed (in literary and poetic terms at least)—passion and sex in Japan could be restored, and provide the children of the next generation the country so desperately seeks.

First published March 8, 2008 in *Asia Times Online*

Thailand's twin threat

The threat is real and the result can be ominous at times. Thailand has a commodity, resource, and forward tactical force that can defeat the most valuable international assets. This "hunter killer" team can ultimately disable any foreign target.

With cunning, they move in orchestrated tandem. In a target-rich environment they split, and seek multiple opportunities. In a target-scarce environment they regroup, compare intelligence and take a consorted approach to a single high-value target.

It is the "twin attack" of Thailand—and they show up in uniform and ready for action.

Da, the elder sister, dons the uniform: spaghetti-strapped babydoll dress over a miniskirt and "fuck me" pump stiletto heels. Fah, her younger "twin", favors a pair of low-rise heels and cuts her hair to match her sister's. Their outfits are always extremely similar.

Hunter-Killer Tactics

Da and Fah are two beautiful women and they are working the bars with an unusual level of skill. The "twins" size up the crowd at a freelance bar in Patpong with an abnormally keen sense of opportunity. They were actually born thirteen months apart, but their strikingly similar physical characteristics make them seem like twins, or at the very least sisters, when working the customers.

Sexy, beautiful women are easy to find in Thailand's sex industry. But sisters, twins or not, are unique and a fetishist's dream. They capitalize on their strikingly similar looks in the sex industry.

"We work together. We are the same," Fah says. "*Farang* want fantasy. We live together, we sleep together and when a *farang* wants it, we have sex together."

"We do," Da says and, never wanting to miss an opportunity, continues, "You want go with sisters?" I twitch and adjust myself on the bar stool.

Sister's Plight

Another bar in Patpong, whose sign and tagline read "Sisters, Take Two", seems interesting in the same vein. However, upon inspection it is a disappointing, tiny bar that claims that daytime hours, businessmen and professionals drive its short-time business.

I ask the *mamasan* if she has any "sisters", but it appears not, despite her arguing: "All of the girls here are sisters."

Although such camaraderie is admirable, one cannot help but be disappointed by the bar's lack of real sisters—is this not false advertising?

On to Soi Cowboy, and the Long Gun go-go bar that does a very convincing lesbian show. The girls look only nominally like each other, but they are sisters and take a similar, focused approach to customers much like their Patpong sisters.

Want one girl? Good. Want two girls? Sisters, twins? Even better.

Barfines remain about the same, averaging about THB400 (US$12.50) per girl. But this is obviously a double barfine that causes the *mamasan* to look on approvingly. Obviously, when dealing with the girls' fees things are slightly inflated. The average short-time cost for a single girl is approximately THB1,000–1,500 (US$31–$47). But with the girls working under the guise of a familial ménage à trois, the price is THB1,500–2,000 (US$47–$62.50) per girl and is generally non-negotiable.

So such an affair could set a punter back some THB4,800 (US$150) for two girls for three hours. Not to mention the cost of a short-time room or a hotel, lady drinks, and possibly food if the ladies are so inclined, which they often are.

Patpong's Twins

Going full circle, we end up back at the noisy Muzik Cafe on the crossroad Soi Crazy Horse that connects Patpong Soi 1 and 2. Wedged between two extremely friendly and flirtatious twins, a writer can slowly glean facts while being fondled and propositioned if the bar tab is open and giving.

Fah, who is seemingly the chattiest of the pair, admits that working about five days per week on average they can make between THB40,000 (US$1,190) and THB100,000 (US$3,000) and per month, depending on a myriad of variables.

No matter the variables, even at their low end of THB40,000 a month they are making more than a college-educated administrative assistant.

"Sometimes we are lazy. Da is very lazy," Fah admonishes while Da pretends to ignore her. "When we get multiple customers, either together or individually, and we make money, Da uses it as an excuse to take a day or two off." Fah is obviously unimpressed by her sister's work ethic.

Da ignores her and homes in on a target of opportunity.

Fah talks a bit more about the work, the pressure, the benefits, the need to do it to make a decent living and support the family, until her sister in arms signals that it is time to execute a consorted attack.

Fah excuses herself with a peck on my cheek and an amorous glare to remind me that if things don't work out with the current target, I might be sighted as a potential replacement.

The somewhat elderly customer is obviously taken by Da, who is the first to approach him. She holds his gaze as her hips gyrate in her micro-miniskirt. He never sees the sneak attack coming that ups the ante in a way that might be impossible to measure.

Fah sidles up behind him and begins massaging his shoulders, but when he attempts to turn to see this new arrival, she covers his eyes and whispers some sort of sweet nothing into his ear. When he is finally allowed to look, he is taken aback to say the least. A moment before he had one of the most beautiful girls in the bar fawning over him—now she seems to have multiplied, along with his luck.

Drinks are bought, very questionable dancing ensues with the *farang* leading his two honeys, and as the bar draws down to its close, the twin tactic is put in play.

"You ever have two ladies, twins, take care of you?" Da coos to the punter.

Before he can answer (he is a bit dumbfounded and buzzed on alcohol at this point), Fah chimes in, "No have customer tonight, I sad!" She feigns depression. "If you take me and sister, very good time, take very good care for you!"

To say that our man, the elderly punter, is akin to a deer in the headlights would be a kind description of the situation.

Minutes later, as the house lights slowly come up signaling the end of yet another evening in Bangkok's red-light district, the fellow, now fully succumbing to the hunter-killer twin team, leaves feeling victorious, with a lady hanging off of each arm.

Nights later they would later tell me in agreement that servicing *farang* together, in tandem, is an easier gig. They even tell me they play a Thai version of the game Rock, Paper, Scissors to decide who initiates vaginal penetrative sex, while the winner simply performs oral duties. Apparently they are good at what they do.

"They [*farang*] come easily with two women. It makes the work easy, sometimes maybe just five minutes," Fah says, pointing out that Da likes to be orally pleased while she takes care of the client.

"So you're a journalist? Hm," Fah considers this for a moment. "I suppose you deserve a discount as this is a story effort."

"My wife is standing over there," I say, pointing. "I don't think she'd appreciate that."

"Bring her along; if two is easy, imagine three," Fah says with a smile. Surprisingly, Da decides to approach my wife and offer their services in a congenial manner. My wife refuses, but decides to leave me with Da and Fah to close the bar down.

Moments later, I receive a text message on my phone. It says simply, "Use a condom." The message is from my wife.

Calling her back immediately, I express that I will be coming home shortly. "Up to you, do what you want. Have fun," she says.

"But...?"

"You've been investigating this for weeks. I am your wife. I don't need to worry, do I? Have fun, but do come home tonight," she concludes, hanging up. Needless to say, I'm dumbfounded.

As we flirt, drink and close down the bar, I press the twins several times. "What the hell did you say to my wife?"

They never told me, and to this day I still wonder; the wife was mute on the subject too. In fact, she never said a word about that night.

Considering the events of the previous days, the history of these women in the bars, and their performance that night, it is obvious that Thailand's twin threat, in terms of the sex industry, is not something to be taken lightly.

When kissing cousins aren't so cute

In an article first published by the London *Sunday Times* this week, Britain's Environment Minister Phil Woolas again cited the dangers of inbreeding in the Pakistani immigrant community in Britain. Appropriately calling it "the elephant in the room", Woolas was careful to point out it was the "Pakistani community"—who just happen to be largely Muslim. Despite choosing his words carefully, Woolas, who served previously as Race Relations Minister, has sparked controversy amongst British Muslims.

Woolas, who represents the ethnically mixed region of Oldham East and Saddleworth, said, "If you talk to any primary care worker they will tell you that levels of disability among the ... Pakistani population are higher than the general population. And everybody knows it's caused by first-cousin marriages. That's a cultural thing rather than a religious thing. It is not illegal in this country."

"The problem is that many of the parents themselves and many of the public spokespeople are themselves products of first-cousin marriages. It's very difficult for people to say 'you can't do that' because it's a very sensitive, human thing," Times Online reported.

The online blogosphere and other newspapers quickly followed the story, often irresponsibly. *Spero* published a similar story titled, "UK minister warns of 'Muslim inbreeding'", even though Woolas said no such thing. That does not seem to matter any longer, though, as the "elephant in the room" has been uncaged.

Bloggers and readers commenting on the story on the Internet quickly took sides and argued about "anti-Muslim politicians" or how all Muslim men want to marry their sister and then give her a beating for good measure. This only served to fan the flames of the controversy, as so many things do these days, and this became a "Muslim" issue. The armchair pundits on both sides were quick and nasty to take sides. Sadly, these vicious, knee-jerk, and oft ill-informed debates shift attention from the real problem.

Interfamily marriages and the resulting inbreeding are found in many societies and cultures all over the world. Several states in the US have passed laws banning interfamily relations or marriage as time and science began to show the resulting genetic problems that it causes. It is not a matter of religion, but a matter of culture and being uninformed of the hazards.

Science has indeed shown that inbreeding within the family will ultimately result in health complications and defects in a propensity of cases. As a result, the United States, at least at a state level, moved to outlaw interfamily marriages for what is considered the individual, familial, public, and social good.

British Pakistanis' interfamily marriages are a concern of public health, due to disproportional representations of birth defects in their population. For British society it puts an added strain on the National Health Service, but short of introducing a law to forbid these marriages, there seems little can be done. The continued attempts to educate people about this seem to have been fruitless thus far.

Woolas is supported by Labour member of Parliament Ann Cryer, who first spoke out on the issue two years ago after research showed British Pakistanis were thirteen times more likely to have children with birth defects than the general population. Cryer told the *Sunday Times*, "This is to do with a medieval culture where you keep wealth within the family."

"I have encountered cases of blindness and deafness. There was one poor girl who had to have an oxygen tank on her back and breathe from a hole in the front of her neck," she added. "The parents were warned they should not have any more children. But when the husband returned from Pakistan, within months they had another child with exactly the same condition."

A possible answer might lie in going to the source of the cultural problem, to Pakistan. A study more than a decade ago found, "The prevalence of interfamily marriages was studied in 940 families belonging to four different socio-economic groups in and around Lahore, Pakistan. The overall prevalence of interfamily marriages was 46%. First-cousin marriages were most common at 67%, followed by marriages between second cousins, 19%."

Marriages between families are often meant to strengthen the bond of kinsmanship. Indeed, women are often more warmly welcomed into the households, less likely to face abuse, and retain some status because they are, well, family. Since this needs to stop, a value—a higher value—must be placed on extra-familial relations and the women it brings into the family—if for nothing more than healthy babies and thus sustain the family bloodline.

The Koran does not have any passages that forbid marrying within the family, and interfamily marriages are documented back to the times of the Prophet Muhammad. Herein lies a possibly more effective solution that actually makes Islam a positive force in this debate.

If Islamic scholars and influential *mullah*s could be presented with evidence of why this practice is bad for their culture, then maybe Sharia Law could be amended. Or at the very least, some of

Islam's most influential *mullah*s in Pakistan could offer guidance to Muslims that would steer families away from this practice.

Meanwhile, media and bloggers that make this a divisive topic based solely on religion ignore the real victims that this problem creates. But perhaps misinformation and religious banter simply make it easier for people to avoid having to take a good hard look at themselves and their culture.

Some may argue that Pakistan is at least a hundred years from a sexual revolution that will increase women's rights, sexual education or reproductive health in their society. What should be more important to everyone is the health of the children, who will carry the future we all seek to protect.

First published February 16, 2008 in *Asia Times Online*

Squeaky clean
in Thailand

Thailand's sex industry is well known for its go-go bars, freelance pick-up joints, and beer gardens. Considering that Thai massage is one of the cornerstones of "Thai Wisdom" (the others being Thai boxing, cooking, and language), it seems only natural that sex and massage would be combined sooner or later.

One such example is the soapy massage. Some places offer a soapy massage on an air-mattress. This is also known as the Bangkok Slide, Full Body Massage, B-Course Massage, Tora Tora Massage etc., and involves lots of suds, full body contact, and titillating interaction. A happy ending is almost a given, whether digital, oral, vaginal, or even anal, and everything is on the menu.

Many men—and even a few women—consider a "soapy" the most delightful and erotic way to spend a couple of hours.

The customer is pampered, undressed, and immersed in a large double bath of warm water. A woman gets in beside the guest and washes him from head to toe with her body, often primarily employing her pubic region as the primary instrument of application. For this reason, this massage has also been dubbed The Brillo in honor of the scrubbing pad, due to the friction of an unshaved, or even shaved, female pubic region.

Lather, bubbles and copious amounts of friction are applied. The women will usually do just about anything for the guest.

Soapy massages usually finish with, at the very least, a happy ending.

Typically when a customer first enters a soapy, he sits down in some type of reception area, has a drink and looks at the ladies. The reception area can range from the likes of a pick-up bar with ladies wandering around chatting up customers, to the "fish bowl" variety where a large glass window separates customers from a selection of women tagged with numbers.

A customer is told to point and choose based on his personal proclivities, or act as a discerning connoisseur and tell the *mamasan* or *papasan* what he'd like. A half dozen girls will then parade for viewing and chatting until the client is satisfied and picks his masseuse. It is at this level of connoisseur or specialty request that a customer can explain to the *mamasan* that he wants a girl to finish him orally, have anal sex, multiple girls, or make other sexual requests that some girls might not be willing to perform.

Money is exchanged—usually about THB1,500 (US$45) to several thousands of baht—and the "treatment" is under way. The customer is lead to a VIP room, many of which have a bath like a hot tub set into the floor that can easily accommodate two to three people (remember, there are customers who choose more than one girl).

Then it is time to relax; the woman will undress the guest and then help him step into the bath, with her following. The customer is washed by the now-naked masseuse and most of the time oral or digital sex ensues.

Then it is time to move to the air mattress where the customer gets the soapy massage. The guest is covered with soap and sponged down while the girl starts to massage him with her body.

During this body massage, the woman will use a particular part of her own body to slither, rub, and grind over just about every inch of his body. Having a women grind her pubic area and vagina over unusual areas of the body—such as neck, calves, and arms—is actually surprisingly erotic, and offers more stimulation (in more ways than one) than you might imagine.

After the massage is finished, there is usually another quick shower with manual and/or oral stimulation. Then it is off to the conveniently equipped and well-placed double, queen- or king-sized bed in the massage room.

From here the guest can choose how to find his own happy ending. The time for all this is normally ninety minutes, but overtime is available and will be billed. For the "classier" establishments there will be no knock at the door, but the bill will be formidable for overtime.

Alternative View

The term "body massage" can be misleading, as one female tourist recently discovered. The *farang* woman was actually traveling with her long-time boyfriend when she decided to visit Phuket for a day of shopping while said boyfriend was scuba diving.

The woman, having already enjoyed the delights of normal non-sexual Thai massages, decided during her trip to take up a lovely Thai girl's offer of a body massage.

Once inside the massage room, our wayward patron realized that something was amiss. "What is a body massage?" she asked. "I just want a massage, full body massage."

To this the Thais considered the question, possibly too literally. Thais are also extremely accepting with homosexuality and bisexuality, which may have further muddied the waters.

"Yes, body massage!" Mamasan proclaimed. "Just beautiful lady, you pick, lady take care of you. Spa! Bath! Soap massage!"

The young female tourist was not deterred. Comfortable with her sexuality, she decided to trudge on. "Her!" she proclaimed, pointing out a rather demure but smiling Thai woman hiding in the shadows.

Our tourist got a soapy and described it as the one of the most erotic experiences in sexuality she has ever experienced. Though she is not a lesbian or even bi-sexual (not before the experience anyway), she described the sexual interaction with the masseuse, that included oral and digital stimulation, as stunning. Also, apparently, grinding the pubic, vaginal region of two female bodies can be fulfilling and exciting.

The satisfied female tourist did say later that most of the soapy was performed, "shower, grinding massage, shower". Much to the consternation of her boyfriend and myself, the details were scant. Thank God the massage girls talk.

"She shaved. And she likes toys, too," the massage girl told me. "I will do girls. But I don't want girls. I have no problem with women, they are sweet and gentle. But it is not the same as having sex a man."

The result, however, was an equally interesting story. The satiated, relaxed, and downright horny female tourist returned to her hotel to await her beau from his day of diving. When he arrived, he was treated to an exceptionally enthusiastic woman who took him for a special shower.

After hours of bubbles, grinding, and writhing in each other's embrace, the exacerbated boyfriend asked what had inspired his long-term girlfriend's performance, as she had not yet relayed the story. The answer was simple Thai Wisdom.

"I just wanted to make sure you were squeaky clean," the woman giggled.

My short time
with Tito

It certainly isn't unusual to find a bunch of eager-looking women working, dancing, or freelancing on the bar scene in East and Southeast Asia. Often these women tend to be of the golden-skinned variety, hailing from Southeast Asia and looking to turn a quick buck. At some clubs in Asia, though, fair-skinned women from the West can also be found plying the sex trade.

In a Southeast Asian town awash with tourists and entertainment zones, one can stumble into a bar where a dozen or so attractive Western women are performing stripper-style dances. Entering the club, it's hard not to recall the strip clubs of the West. And it's not just the girls. The style of the show is also the same: one girl dances on a small stage, strips down to just a thong, and then makes a round of the bar, lap-dancing for each of the patrons hoping for a tip. Certainly, this is not the standard fare of go-go bars in Asia.

One particular bar I visited had a truly Western touch; between sets, idle ladies were sitting looking sullen, self-absorbed, and studiously ignoring the customers.

In an effort to learn more, I sought the company of one of the young women. My initial approach was immediately met with a convincing "die in a fire" look of scorn. But when a drink was offered, her mood seemed to lighten. I soon discovered why a lady drink in this place costs so much more (about US$10, which is hardly comparable to many local places that charge no more than US$3).

The girl assured me that she got to keep half. "It is one of the ways we make money here," she said. "Girls dance about one set per hour. There are private rooms in the back for private shows. It is [US$30] per five songs, per girl. To take a girl out of the bar it is [US$60] for two hours." In comparison, this would get a guy two locals for an all-night stay—with no holds barred.

When asked about arrangements outside the bar, the svelte, leggy blonde was aghast. "Sex? No way!" she said. "If a guy wants to [have sex] he can go find a local girl for 'boom-boom'."

Delicate prying—and more plying with drinks—soon gleaned more personal facts. The attractive blonde's name was Dasha. She was twenty-one years old and originally from Ukraine, where she was a college student, but low on cash. "I can come to work in Asia for a year and save up enough for another year of university, I hope," said Dasha.

A friend in Ukraine had referred her to an "agent" and soon she was on "the circuit". Attractive women like Dasha are ferried around East and Southeast Asia on a circuit strongly influenced by organized crime groups such as the Russian mafia, Japan's Yakuza, and Chinese triad gangs. The top money-making stops are Japan, Hong Kong, Macau, and Singapore, while stops in the rest of Southeast Asia or mainland China are layovers, places to wait for a new visa needed to get back to the higher-earning ports of call.

"Girls are from all over: one is from Georgia, another from Lithuania, two girls are from Ukraine, like me. Oh, and Olga is from Russia," Dasha said, pointing to the sexy brunette gyrating around a pole in only a pair of heels and a G-string.

"Japan is the best. Even without sex the men will pay thousands just for your company, to tease them," she said. "But if you are one of the girls who are reluctant to [have sex] it can be harder to earn decent money in other places."

Dasha estimated that she would earn several thousand US dollars from her thirty-day stint in this Southeast Asia club, but was looking forward to greener pastures. Eventually, she revealed some details about the sexual aspects of her work. "First answer is no, but some of the girls will have sex with the customers. I'd consider it. If I can feel some sort of physical attraction to the guy, then maybe."

"The girls can choose who they go with, no one forces them, the bodyguards look after us," she continued while pointing out a bulky fellow near the door with no neck and enormous arms, who now seemed to raise his brow a bit as he realized he was somehow the topic of conversation. "It is up to the girl what she wants to charge, but most wouldn't dream of going with a customer for less than US$500."

Dasha suddenly stopped talking, seemingly bored with the conversation, and with my research completed—and the fact that the bruiser by the door was taking more of an interest in our exchange—I paid the bill and made for the exit. With much relief, I noted that the bar-room Neanderthal was nowhere to be seen.

Outside I was not so lucky. At the base of the stairway, the bouncer rounded the corner and blocked my path. "I want talk. Let's go for walk," he said in unspectacular English. My efforts at protesting were met with frustration. "I ask you to talk, nothing else. If I want to hurt you, I hurt you here. You think anyone care? Now, come." The bouncer gestured for me to follow.

After half a block of weaving through the crowd, the nearest road came into view and I immediately noticed two equally big bruisers on Harley Davidsons—not totally unusual, but rare in this country. When the men started their engines, I knew they'd been waiting for us.

"I thought you said we were taking a walk," I said lightly.

"Yes, we walk motorcycle, go ride. Come, get on," the bouncer said.

The ride was short—five minutes or so—and took me to a part of the town I was unfamiliar with, but still with a number of pubs and restaurants. We stopped in front of a place that had a sign in Cyrillic text.

The riders hung back, allowing the bouncer and I to enter the establishment on our own. A few glances and a cold stare at me from at least one patron were all that greeted us. Making our way to a private table at the rear, the bouncer nodded once or twice and said, "*Das ve dania*" as he greeted several patrons.

The dimly lit nightclub was swarming with beautiful Western women wearing only thongs. There was no pretense of stripping: women walked around, settled around tables, chatted with customers, and sharing drinks with them, all while nearly or completely nude. The atmosphere was very similar to Japanese hostess clubs, less the nudity part of it, of course.

Once settled at a table, the burly bouncer said, "It is private club," and dismissively waved a hand at the scene. "Who are you? What are you doing at club, asking girls questions?"

After a few awkward and increasingly tense explanations, the bouncer, whose name turned out to be Tito, seemed satisfied that I was no harm and even began to give suggestions: "Don't name the bar," he recommended. "Or even the country."

As Tito loosened up, he had some mostly naked girls join us and ordered a bottle of Russian moonshine to do shots from—no chaser offered. He even began to disclose details about the so-called circuit of Western sex workers in Asia. "The house makes 50% of what girl makes," he said. "But we give them place sleep, food to eat, and arrange their air tickets and visas."

"Fifty percent?" I asked, possibly a little too affected by the moonshine. "Seems a bit high."

Tito regarded me with a scowl. "It's fair, trust me."

He went on to confirm that the house is also entitled to a 50% cut of the money the girls make outside the bar from sex.

"But how do you know what each girl is charging every time she goes out?" I asked. "The price seems to vary."

"We know. It does vary, yes," Tito said, looking at me as though he was considering if I was a bit daft. "They give us half."

Three or four mostly naked women fawned over us, pouring drinks, lighting cigarettes, and generally rubbing and groping. This bar seemed to provide the drinks to the girls for free when asked. Tito would occasionally peel a large denomination of local currency off a wad in his pocket and hand the bill to a girl or slip it in her G-string, when she was actually wearing one. I tried to do this but he waved me off of it after seeing me do it a couple times, explaining that it was a private club and I was a guest.

I asked about how some of the girls apparently didn't go for sex. This drew a surprised look from Tito, then he thought for a moment, finally saying, "Ah, Dasha," with a laugh. "She plays hard to get, and is good at getting top price. You like Dasha?"

I did, of course. She was stunning, and I answered, "Of course, she is gorgeous!"

Tito smiled and barked something in Russia to one of the bikers who had settled himself by the door with an attractive brunette rubbing herself up against him. He downed his shot, gave his companion a light smack on the ass to shoo her away, and was out the door, followed by the roar of a Harley screaming into the night. Of the words Tito had barked at him, I had only understood the word "Dasha".

"I don't want to get her in trouble!" I said, a bit alarmed. Tito assured me everything was fine and that the girls actually like hanging out at the private club, where they draw a base salary, tips, and are allowed to drink freely so long as they don't get too drunk.

Sure enough twenty minutes later, during which I convinced the lovely girl next to me to get me a glass of water before the moonshine burned a hole in my stomach (which resulted in a look from her, obviously questioning my manhood), Dasha arrived with the biker, who retook his seat by the door with his nude female companion.

Dasha looked surprised and a little confused as she approached Tito's (no doubt) regular table, noticing me sitting with him and a few girls. She was in cute street clothes consisting of a button-down blouse tied at the midsection, showing off her muscled, toned abdomen, and a pair of cut-off "Daisy Duke" jeans that accentuated her long legs.

"*Das ve dania,*" she said. Both Tito and I answered in kind, confusing her even more. Tito said something and I gathered that she was off to get "changed".

Minutes later she emerged from a back room completely naked, and I can report that it was a glorious effect. She did not seem in the least bit self-conscious and had little reason to be. The loose T-shirt and hot pants she'd worn in the other club while she'd waited for her next dance had done little to show off her beauty.

She approached me, staring seductively with a faint smile as I took in her buoyant C-cup breasts and the thin patch of golden pubic hair extending up from her otherwise shaved pussy; utterly magnificent.

"You like? I can sit with you?" Dasha said, asking the obvious. Meanwhile, the girl next to me slid away, making room for Dasha to sit closer to me.

She asked me something in Russian. Before I realized that she was asking if I spoke Russian, she reverted to English. "You speak Russian? You greeted me in Russian?" I told her I didn't speak the language, only a few phrases.

The night rolled on, and the drinks flowed. I kept one hand protectively near my glass of water while the other was delightfully taken by Dasha and placed palm down on her soft pubic hair, where she held it firmly, gently massaging it over her vulva and occasionally pressing one of my or both of our fingers into her vagina. She would moan softly in my ear, rub her breasts against me, and sometimes stroke the now rock-hard presence in my pants. Tito grew boisterous with drinks, women, Russian music, and telling stories (mostly in Russian, which Dasha would give me basic subtitles for). My comrade sporadically slapped me on the back so hard that I thought it would adjust my spine.

"So you got me out of the bar after all," Dasha said at one point. "You surprise me. I wonder what other surprises you have for me." She bit her lip seductively and gripped my crotch a bit harder.

As the night drew to a close, and on wobbly legs, I graciously accepted a ride at the insistence of my new friend Tito. He shared with me one last nugget of knowledge—one I won't soon forget: "Never screw your friends."

First published March 21, 2008 in *Asia Times Online*

Thailand produces the world's smallest porn star

She hails from Udon Thani in Thailand's Northeast, an area known as Isaan, but also famous for its poverty, rice farming, and beautiful women. These women often constitute the majority of the girls working the bars in the sex industry tourist haunts of Bangkok, Pattaya, and Phuket.

One particular teenaged Isaan girl has, by choosing to work in pornography and being a mere 134 cm (4'5") tall and weighing only 32.9 kg (72.5 lbs), gained the title of "world's smallest porn star".

Some basic research into the subject seems to prove that the appropriately stage named "Thainee", with stats of 74B-54-70 cm (28B-21-27"), is in fact the world's smallest porn star—at least of the non-midget variety.

Even former adult star and Vivid contract girl Kobe Tai, (a.k.a. Carla Carter, Clara Scott, Blake Young, and Brooke Young), of Taiwanese decent and loved for her petite figure seems statuesque and portly at 81B-55-81 cm (32B-22-32"), 41 kg (90 lbs) and 160 cm (5'3") when compared to Thainee.

Adult Career

She made her adult career debut, albeit of the amateur variety, about two months ago via her website www.thainee.com. Thainee does the full gamut in her porn performances, from still photography to hardcore gonzo/POV-style male-female sex scenes.

Though she is new to the scene, she appears to have been quite busy in her purported eighteenth year of age, producing hundreds of photographs from dozens of photo shoots and a few dozen more videos for her website.

Asian Sex Gazette recently had the opportunity to speak with Thainee in an exclusive interview.

Thainee, who turned eighteen in April this year, was raised in Kanchanaburi Province, thirty minutes outside of Udon Thani, near the Laos border. Sadly, her parents died when she was young, and she moved to Pattaya when she was eleven to live with her aunt who runs a beauty salon.

Living in Pattaya did have positive effects though. When asked about the sex industry in terms of prostitution, she says, "I learned about the entertainment business through the many girls who came to our shop every day. They spoke of good and bad stories, but I was too scared to ever try."

So how did she get into modeling and pornography? "I was approached while shopping one day by a man who asked if I was interested in doing modeling. I said no at first, but after a lengthy discussion I decided that it would be exciting."

"I love getting to travel around the country and stay at really nice hotels. I love the beach and many of the locations have been in remote parts of Thailand," she says, pointing out some of the advantages to her career.

Besides the fringe benefits there is, of course, the money factor that makes adult modeling and pornography an enticing career move. Thainee explains, "So far it's more money than I've ever seen in my life. I hope to have my own beauty salon someday. And everything during the production has been free. I get to keep the clothes and I have a really nice mobile phone, plus all the travel expenses were paid too." She speaks enthusiastically, immediately adding, "I have a really nice apartment and a new motorbike but they (her producers and co-star 'boyfriend') took away my keys because I had a few accidents already. They think I'm too tiny for it so now it sits outside doing nothing." She trails off in resignation.

Her website has been doing quite well since its debut. Thainee also adds that she was paid an initial fee and gets a lifetime percentage of the profits from her website. She also notes, "I don't know how many members I have but I think it's already a few thousand. I am spending more and more time answering emails every day."

Thainee.com is run by an American organization out of Florida that protect their anonymity. It also runs numerous other Thai feature girl pornography sites. Models Tussinee, Tailynn, and Lulu are also produced by the same company and range from softcore to hardcore. Thainee is decidedly hardcore. All of the companies' websites block access from within Thailand to avoid scrutiny by the authorities.

The pornography that they produce in Thainee's case is clearly illegal under Thai law. Both Thainee and her producers and boyfriend would face prosecution. While the penalties are usually comparatively minor for the Thai women involved, the *farang* boyfriend/co-star and producers would face a jail term, a substantial fine, and be blacklisted from traveling to Thailand.

The petite size that has made Thainee the world's smallest porn star wasn't always an asset in terms of dating. "I don't have many men speak to me, maybe because they think I am still thirteen or something," Thainee says, pointing out that she only had one Thai boyfriend prior to meeting her co-star and now boyfriend.

"I was then introduced to my boyfriend at the end of April,"

Thainee says. "He works for the company that makes my website. I feel very comfortable having sex with him and we have a great time together."

I was a bit perplexed because when I investigated the site I found that the domain name was registered in early 2006—at a time when Thainee would have been only seventeen. This was explained away by a company representative who said that they registered the name in the hopes of finding a girl to fit the stage name.

Thainee is, of course, a stage name. "My real name is long and like most [Thai] models in my profession, stage names are invented that represent a character or personality. I think they were searching for a tiny girl and the ironic part is that for many years I have heard foreigners refer to me as Tiny. So I believe it was a perfect match!" Thainee explains.

Also disclosing her real name would put her at risk of being successfully tracked down and prosecuted by the police. All of the models working for the veiled and security-conscious American company are using assumed names. Indeed, relying rather heavily on the sex-tourist haven of Pattaya has proved a challenge for Thainee and her producers.

A recent shoot was easily identified as having taken place at the Penthouse Hotel in Pattaya. The police put the squeeze on the management to provide whatever information they could about the porn troupe. Luckily for Thainee and her gang, they'd been smart enough not to walk in carrying cameras, lights, and signs proclaiming "Porn production—Staff only", so the management had little to offer police. Remembering one specific couple is quite a challenge given that the hotel is frequented by a constant bevy of sex tourists and nubile young Thai girls from the bustling local sex industry.

Thainee's co-star boyfriend has also been smart enough to

never allow his face to appear on camera, so a positive identification would have to be made using less conventional methods.

Concluding our discussion about her new career, Thainee summarizes by saying, "I didn't choose pornography, pornography chose me. I was just working in a beauty salon dreaming of something better when a man introduced me to something that sounded really fun. I never even saw a sex video until I started making them. I do what comes natural to me and making love to my boyfriend is natural. I don't really consider it being a porn movie or that people will watch it." She adds with a laugh, "I didn't even know what a porn star was!"

Still, Thainee is an oversized hit as the world's smallest porn star.

Asia's dangerous emperor syndrome

Many people felt deep sympathy for Japanese Princess Kiko; she found herself under relentless and stunning pressure to bear a baby boy as an heir to the Emperor. This has long been a majestic male-centric interpretation of familial ideals. The idea of carrying on the family name through a male heir is not lost in Western culture, but the far reaching and negative effect it is having on some Asian societies is proving to be both sad and dangerous.

However, producing an heir, especially a male heir, should not be the sole responsibility of the woman—infertility can result from either partner. Not forgetting, of course, the most basic and well-established scientific truth that it is the male sperm, with its either X or Y chromosome, that determines the gender of the baby.

In a joyous and rightfully deserved outcome, Princess Kiko became pregnant in 2006 and after much anticipation, on September, 6 2006 she bore a boy named Hisahito, amid much celebration both within the royal family and throughout Japan.

Japan's Princess Kiko is a single example of the pressure sometimes placed upon women to produce a male heir. In that case in was in an effort to guarantee the continuation of the monarchy, but Japanese society at large does not have a preference for male babies.

By contrast, it is the two most populated countries in the world where cultural and societal issues are causing gender discrimination. For decades, China and India have had a preference for male offspring, and both countries are now suffering from a disproportionate gender ratio.

The United Nations Development Program (UNDP) reported as recently as 2006 that the female to male birth ratio is believed to be 850:1000 in China, while a 2001 report and census in India found the ratio to be 927:1000. While these are national averages, provincial or state-level numbers can be even more dismal. For example, in India's state of Haryana the same report found the ratio to be 820:1000.

Overall, some experts believe that as many at three million female fetuses are terminated through gender-selective abortions each year in China and India. The long-term effect of these lost females can be devastating, both socially and economically.

The reasons for preferring males are unique and vary between the two countries. In China there is strong familial pressure to produce a baby boy to carry on the family name; this has been exacerbated by China's "one child policy" that was implemented in 1979. The aim of the one child policy was to stem the exploding population in China, and though this may have helped a bit (at least in having a lot less females), the side effects have been abandoned baby girls, female infanticide, and gender-selective abortions.

China has tried to reverse this trend in recent years by allowing a couple having a girl as their first child to be exempted from the rule, offering subsidies to families having a female child and further subsidies should the second child be a female too.

India has similar issues driving the preference for baby boys, even without any government-mandated population controls. One of the foremost issues, it seems, isn't so much a preference for baby boys, but instead a bias against baby girls. India practices a sort of "reverse dowry". Typically, in societies that practice the dowry system, the male and sometimes his family provide a dowry of money and presents for the bride and her family. In India, however, the responsibility of providing a dowry is on the female and her family, and can often be quite extensive and costly. In a country where poverty remains an issue, it is easy to see why the perceived burden of having a daughter might make some families think twice.

At the same time in India, like China, the preference for male children is important in matters such as carrying on a family name. In addition, both societies believe that a male child will be more capable of supporting the family as the parents grow old. As a result, India suffers similar problems to China: female babies face abortion, abandonment, or infanticide.

And just as in China, India has taken similar steps in trying to reverse the trend. The government outlawed the dowry system but unfortunately it is still widely practiced as it is seen as a cultural tradition. The government also hands out subsidies for female children. Both China and India have outlawed gender-selective abortions, yet it is still widely practiced.

Whether abandoned at birth or raised by their parents for some years, many girls in these countries face exploitation in the sex industry. Sometimes even the parents sell their children into the industry to rid themselves of the burden of an unwanted daughter and mitigate the poverty they suffer through the money gained by selling a daughter.

A lack of females in both countries has also created a generation of desperate bachelors. The side effect of this is a boom in prostitution, sexual assaults, and rape cases as men lack sexual outlets, and the ability to find a companion or wife.

While each family is no doubt selfishly assuming that some

other family will provide a princess for their precious little emperor, the sad reality is that both Chinese and Indian men are finding it increasingly difficult to find their match.

"The authorities are shocked at the bride shortage in [India], and they are suddenly clamping down in a big way," said Richa Tanwar, director of women's studies at Kurukshetra University in Haryana, speaking to the *Times of India*. "But even the bride shortage is not going to change things in [our] society ... The attitude is 'Okay, let the neighbors have daughters, I still want my sons.'"

Sons are believed to be an economic asset, while daughters are a liability, and these attitudes are nothing new to South Asia. It is not beyond parents to murder females, either by suffocating them, starving them, or giving them a fatal dose of opium.

Both India and China, along with many countries in Asia, need to increase the perception and value of females in society. They are the mothers, sisters, and daughters that should be cherished; they are also the embodiment through which the next generation of sons and daughters will be produced.

Women throughout much of Asia are becoming increasingly successful and often just as able to help support their families as their male counterparts. Ensuring healthcare, education, and opportunities through education—which both countries have started campaigns to provide—will help to insure the success of the next generation of females, and the progress of the societies themselves; it alleviates the social and economic woes that the gender gap is creating.

Maybe Chinese and Indian couples just need to be reminded that the daughter they might have could become the next top Bollywood actress, or famed Canto-pop singer, Miss India or China, Sonia Ghandi, a powerful party member of the central government, a doctor who saves lives, a woman who gives

.inspiration or, at the very least but no less admirable, the mother of their grandchildren.

It would be wrong to take away such potential without even giving her a chance.

Cell swingers in Cambodia

Considering the glacial legal wrangling, domestic indifference, and rampant allegations of corruption and mismanagement, some might say it's about time sex came up at the Khmer Rouge tribunal, now under way in the Kingdom of Cambodia.

The ultra-Maoist group's former supremo and "Brother No 1", Pol Pot, died in 1998 in a hidden jungle redoubt along the Thai border. His infamous military doyen Ta Mok, dubbed "The Butcher" by the Western press, passed away suspiciously in a Phnom Penh military hospital in 2006. With the most atrocious and eye-catching suspects out of the picture, and the rest of the leadership clique enjoying decades of leisure and, in one case, even a royal pardon, the United Nations-sponsored tribunal has been a stop-start, anticlimactic affair of official rhetoric and obtuse legalese.

For journalists embedded in the turgid trial process it's been a long, boring slog.

And so it was on February 25 that local media reported that former Khmer Rouge "Brother No 3", eighty-two-year-old Ieng Sary, had requested that the court grant him conjugal visits with his wife—and fellow court detainee—Khieu Thirith. In the history of international justice, dating back to the Nuremberg Trials of the late 1940s, this must surely be the only time two suspects, both charged with crimes of atrocity and both in custody, have asked for a little tete-a-tete. Remember, too, the elderly couples' autumn incarceration, and any potential jail-cell rendezvous, are all courtesy of the UN, the taxpayers of its contributing member states, and the millions of Cambodians victimized by the murderous regime.

To explain the plea, *The Cambodia Daily*, a Phnom Penh-based media NGO, reported Ieng Sary's lawyer Ang Udom as saying the octogenarian "misses his wife". "He wants to see her, she wants to see him ... why does the tribunal prevent them from seeing each other?" the paper quoted Ang Udom as saying.

To add irony to insult, Sary and Thirith, who was the Khmer Rouge's social affairs minister, both set policies for the Khmer Rouge, a significant plank of which was to dismantle the traditional family structure. Husbands, wives, and children were separated into gender-based work collectives. Marriages were routinely forced on individuals simply for reproduction to ensure a productive workforce.

Kalyanee Mam wrote in *The Endurance of the Cambodian Family Under the Khmer Rouge Regime: An Oral History* that: "Marriages were usually forced upon individuals for reproductive purposes only, since most couples who were married were soon after separated from each other and rarely met afterwards. After reproduction was achieved, it was not important for couples to remain together, since their time and energy were required on the work field."

Almost thirty years have passed since the end of the Khmer Rouge's horrific rule from 1975–1979, during which as many as one in five Cambodians were killed. Many more were tortured or died of disease or starvation in the forced labor camps of agriculture collectives in which the entire population was enslaved.

The Extraordinary Chambers in the Courts of Cambodia, established by a 2001 law and convened in 2006, was initially scheduled to last three years and cost US$56.3 million, with the UN providing US$43 million and Cambodia's government US$13.3 million. But money problems have plagued the court, and Agence France Presse reported recently that the court was seeking another US$114 million from international donors to keep it going until 2011. The majority of Cambodians live on less than US$1 per day.

Former foreign minister Ieng Sary, and former social affairs minister Thirith, seventy-five, are in custody alongside Khieu Samphan, seventy-six, the former head of state, "Brother No 2" Nuon Chea and Duch, the warden of the notorious torture center known as S-21, or Tuol Sleng. They are being held separately in eight privately housed single-room cells in a detention facility on the same property as the courtroom on the outskirts of Phnom Penh. They all deny charges of war crimes or crimes against humanity.

Sary is suspected of undertaking and facilitating murders, as well as planning and coordinating Khmer Rouge policies of forcible transfer, forced labor, and illegal killings. Thirith was allegedly one of the planners who directed the widespread purges and the killings of members within the Ministry of Social Affairs. Both have claimed they are innocent.

The mere thought of a request for conjugal visits between Sary and Thirith is a shocking insult to Cambodians. However, in another universe it might be touching. The couple met during their university days in Phnom Penh where they surely double-dated with fellow classmates Pol Pot and his future wife Khieu Ponnary, Thirith's sister. They were married in the summer of 1951 in Paris, where Sary had a flat in the Latin Quarter and a coterie of radical student friends, many of whom were expatriate Cambodian communists. According to historian Ben Kiernan, Thirith was a "Shakespeare studies major".

Sary rose to power alongside his chum Pol Pot, and ultimately became deputy prime minister of Democratic Kampuchea, as the Khmer Rouge named the country. After their 1979 ousting, and a Hanoi-backed tribunal that same year, which sentenced Sary to death in absentia, the Khmer Rouge fought a guerrilla war against the government into the 1990s. Sary became the first senior Khmer Rouge leader to defect to the government in 1996. At the behest of Prime Minister Hun Sen, King Norodom Sihanouk issued a royal pardon to Sary later that year and granted him semi-autonomous status in the gem- and timber-rich municipality of Pailin, where his son is now governor. Sary and Thirith have lived in an opulent Phnom Penh villa for many years.

Sary's amnesty was a stumbling block in the lengthy negotiations between the Cambodian government and the UN and served to stall its progress.

Even with recent developments, decades of delays have created apathy among the Cambodian populace. As Khmer Rouge survivor and famous painter Vann Nath told an Asia Times Online staffer in November 2007, "It has taken too long for the trial. It has dragged on for years and now as the delays of the trial keep going there will be more ways to defend the suspects—and more delays."

Nath, who was one of only a handful of survivors of S-21, points out that the leaders in custody certainly have better living conditions than those who suffered at their hands. "They're secure, they have mattresses, any food they want, special doctors," he said. "They have better luck than most Cambodians."

If Sary's luck continues, he might just get his conjugal visits. But he's been hospitalized three times with heart problems since his arrest in December 2007, and it's doubtful the tender reunion of these two war crimes suspects would be exceedingly risqué (although Americans may remember the *Seinfeld* episode in which character George Costanza reckoned conjugal visits to be the best sex possible).

Or, perhaps, the scales of justice are tipping in mysterious ways. As far-fetched a scenario as it may be, should Sary go out with a bang in some Khmer Rouge tribunal jail cell, it would certainly spark interest in what has been an otherwise impotent process.

First published March 1, 2008 in *Asia Times Online*

The young ones

In Japan, the practice of an older man taking a young, school-aged Japanese girl out on a "date" in exchange for money is referred to as *enjo kosai*, or "compensated dating". To say that *enjo kosai* is prostitution or, in a Western view, child prostitution may not always be accurate, as the date may not necessarily include sex. At the same time it is a cultural complexity that can strain local and international perceptions of the practice.

Enjo kosai does not automatically imply that sex is on offer. In some cases the date could be just dinner, conversation, and maybe a walk holding hands. All too often, though, it does involve some sort of sexual interaction, maybe limited to fondling and groping, or oral sex and full sexual intercourse. This then does raise concerns about child prostitution, at least in the eyes of the international community, as the schoolgirls who are providing this service can be as young as twelve.

A svelte twenty-year-old Japanese girl named Aiko, who was working the bars in Hong Kong "for a lark" while on "holiday", as she put it—because she didn't need to, she assured me—said she had been doing *enjo kosai* since she was fourteen. "Why not? it's there. There are Japanese men willing to pay good money for nothing more than a tease. I could make huge money and get designer brands just for having dinner at a five-star restaurant and being his date," Aiko said. She continued, "If they later wanted sex, which in Japan is all about the tease and being unattainable, then that just makes the man invest more money in the relationship."

Aiko is an educated, upper-middle-class woman.

In Japan, a country where the age of sexual consent is twelve, one of the lowest in the world (in metro Tokyo at least, whereas the national average is fourteen years old in the provinces), the practice of having sex with girls of this age group is not illegal. If the girl says "yes", then a man of any age can take her for sex. This is where *enjo kosai* acts a loophole, because if a girl of this age group says "yes, for 50,000 yen (US$477)", then immediately the situation is illegal, with the male customer taking the brunt of the punishment for being involved in solicitation and prostitution, aggravated by the fact that she's a minor (under eighteen in terms of recent legislation).

This is exactly where the loophole becomes a pedophile's, or in this case salaryman's, dream scenario. If he "dates" the underage girl, buys her gifts, and occasionally provides her with sums of cash on the side for her to shop, buy books, or have a good time with friends, then the money and gifts are not technically—very technically, and absurdly—provided in relation to a sex-for-money prostitution-based transaction.

Neither is the transaction as commercially straightforward as it is in Bangkok or Manila, where a client can pay by the hour for sex, even if he and his hired partner don't share a common language. In Japan, the girls set their own rates, but it is certainly correct to say that dinner and a movie come cheaper than the cost of a roll in the hay at a local love hotel. Beyond this, the girls involved in *enjo kosai* also usually expect to be taken shopping and lavished with designer goods, especially by men they date repeatedly.

Some, but certainly not all, of the girls working the *enjo kosai* trade are referred to as *kogal*s, a term which takes its meaning from the Japanese word *kou*, meaning "high", and *gyaru*, meaning "girl". Some have compared them to the American Valley Girl phenomenon of the 1980s. Donning the schoolgirl uniform, hip designer goods, and top-of-the-line mobile phones, these girls are stereotyped as being drug users, promiscuous, greedy, and stupid, all at the same time. Apparently this stereotyping is not without basis. The girls like trendy hangouts, such as Tokyo's Ikebukuro district, where they can eat, shop, chat with friends, sing karaoke, and maybe land a salaryman for a date.

As stated, *kogal*s are not the only subculture participating in *enjo kosai*, but they make up a significant portion and certainly are the poster girls of the practice. But any schoolgirl participating in the trade is practicing *enjo kosai*. There are no pimps or *mamasan*s setting up the liaisons, but Japan has a host of pay-to-play—for the male's benefit anyway—phone and Internet matchmaking services to facilitate hook-ups of like-minded individuals.

"I was never a *kogal*," Aiko said with disdain. "*Yarinige*, *oyaji-gari*. It's crap!" (The word *yarinige* means a situation where a man fails to pay his promised debts for services rendered, while *oyaji-gari* is an encounter where schoolgirls plan a heist with an unsuspecting salaryman as their victim. Both these terms are largely a part of the *kogal* subculture.)

A foreigner has little chance of entering the world of *enjo kosai* unless he is fluent in Japanese and familiar with the cultural nuances that the relationship requires.

However, despite the hype in the media and pornography industry, these schoolgirls of Japan are probably not as common as one is led to believe. Foreigners are extremely unlikely to have an *enjo kosai* experience, and sex with Japanese schoolgirls is likely to remain simply a twisted fantasy for most visitors to Japan. The most common way for foreigners to obtain sex for money in Japan by paying imported Thai and Filipino girls at inflated Japanese rates—most Japanese clubs with Japanese girls do not allow foreigners in.

As previously noted, sex in exchange for money is illegal in Tokyo, but in 2005 the city moved to make the practice of *enjo kosai* illegal, with penalties that could land the man in jail for up to a year. However, gathering the evidence necessary to successfully prosecute seems dicey, and few reports over the past few years suggest that it is being vigorously enforced.

The only reports of enforcement seem to surround mostly teachers, doctors, or men in similar positions of authority who use their weight to gain sexual favors from the girls in their charge. Technically, though, this does not fall under the *enjo kosai* heading of enforcement as the men are not dating or paying the girls, but instead coercing them. To Japan's credit, at least these types of sexual relationships with minors are increasingly being prosecuted.

Enjo kosai is more accepted than one might expect, the most recent citation, a decade old, by the *Tokyo Weekender* stated, "According to a recent survey of junior high-school students in their final year, 17% thought there is nothing wrong with *enjo kosai* and 13% replied that they felt no reluctance in practicing it."

In another citation sometime in April, 1998, the daily *Mainichi* conducted a survey and found: "Despite extravagant media attention on what many had perceived to be a widespread phenomenon, only 5% of high schoolgirls admitted taking part in *enjo kosai*—accepting money from middle-aged men for dates that sometimes include having sexual intercourse."

As we have witnessed in many areas of sexuality, these numbers will only have increased a decade later; the media's focus on sex, increased ability to communicate easily, and the Internet which, through pornography, seems to be able to shift the moral barriers of youth, has inevitability led to a more open view of sex and sexuality among youths throughout the world.

Another problem with the *enjo kosai* "industry" is that the number of prospective punters far outnumber the amount of willing schoolgirls. Some estimates have put the number of school-aged girls practicing *enjo kosai* at about 13%, while a Tokyo survey by *Friday* magazine found that an astonishing 75% of schoolgirls reported that they had been solicited by older men seeking an *enjo kosai* relationship.

For non-Japanese observers, understanding the cultural context of *enjo kosai* can be challenging, especially when trying to rationalize this practice against their own views on sex, prostitution, and the law.

The *Asahi Shimbun* newspaper found, through interviewing girls in the *enjo kosai* trade, that many do so as a reaction to their own fathers' behavior. Many men are slaves to the long hours of a salaryman's job, and many men exacerbate these long hours by going out drinking at hostess clubs, having sex in soaplands, and returning home late and drunk, only to repeat the process the next day. Many of the girls involved in *enjo kosai* think their fathers probably have their own *kogal*s anyway, so why shouldn't they also reap the rewards of the practice?

Societies all over the world struggle with issues like prostitution and underage sex, sometimes with absurd and sad results. For example, in the US, despite a relatively recent sexual revolution in the 1960s and 1970s, puritan and conservative laws still seem to rule the day. Laws that somewhat arbitrarily define an adult as being over eighteen and thus anyone below as a minor, and prohibit sexual interaction between these two age groups, are vigorously enforced. Sometimes, with the sad result of prosecuting an eighteen- or nineteen-year-old man for having sex with his long-time girlfriend, who may be only sixteen or seventeen, and thus creating a victim and a predator where there were neither.

Then there is the "teacher problem" that further demonstrates the difficulties in trying to legislate and enforce sexual boundaries based on age. In what has become almost daily news, teachers— and in many cases attractive female teachers—are being arrested and prosecuted for sex with their students. Given that these minors are hormone-addled teenage boys, they are almost always willing, and enthusiastic, participants. While the law seems rigid on enforcement, society and the media have not failed to notice that, while men labeled as predators in similar situations are harshly punished, the women seem to get off (pun intended) with much lighter sentences.

With so much debate over victims and predators, one can't help but wonder which is the more enlightened society: the US and countries in the West criminalizing sex, or a country like Japan that does not prosecute when there are not clear victims? In any situation where there is not consent, or there is an abuse of authority and coercion exists, then the case should be prosecuted. Surely any sexual contact with a person twelve years of age or under should be vigorously prosecuted as what it is: pedophilia.

Considering that Japan had a rather early sexual revolution during the Edo Period in the seventeenth century, we can only wonder how the sexual revolutions sweeping across Asia in recent decades will affect the future. As a leading industrialized nation and international trade partner, Japan has bent to the will of the international community and updated or created laws, mostly concerning child pornography. It has also tentatively ventured into the realm of creating laws regarding underage sex, though enforcement is still lax on both.

Will Japan's eastern neighbors adopt similar views on youth sex, or will they bend to the influence of the West to legislate youth sex after the sexual awaking of their societies? We can only wait and see, and hope that creating victims and predators where there are none in the realm of sexuality throughout the world is limited to where victims actually exist.

First published May 10, 2008 in *Asia Times Online*

Bedding burlesque babes in Burma

The social, political, and economic struggles Burma has weathered over recent decades have led to an unforeseen increase in women opting to work in the sex industry in an effort to escape poverty. Once confined to a small domestic market, the sex trade is opening up to the still small but emerging tourist industry.

While it might be common in many parts of Asia, in Burma prostitution dens of working girls were comparatively rare just a decade ago. Both extreme poverty and lack of other opportunities are making more and more young women turn to the sex trade that exists in karaoke bars, massage parlors, nightclubs, and restaurants.

The military junta has mismanaged the country for decades, not to mention sanctions that crippled the country during the post-Indochina war years. The regime took control, chose socialism, and then made promises of democratic reform that never materialized, drawing angst and sanctions from many in the international community.

In 1996 the military, perhaps sensing that things weren't going so well, decided to ditch socialism for a market economy. However, they apparently failed to realize that in a country still under the thumb of military rule and sanctions, the glowing, positive effects they hoped for would be hard to achieve. With no more

WILLIAM SPARROW

of the equality that had come from socialism, entrepreneurism, opportunism, and individualism naturally took hold. In one of the world's poorest nations, prostitution naturally boomed under such conditions.

In a country where civil servants, police officers, and average workers make 20,000 kyats (US$17) a month and struggle to survive on that, it is understandable that women turn to the sex trade. Like in many Southeast Asian countries, a girl can make in one night the equivalent of an average month's wage working as a prostitute—servicing foreigners, anyway.

"The basic [monthly] salary is similar to what I earned at a factory, but here we get tips from customers," a working girl told AFP in a recent report. "Sometimes we earn 30,000 kyats in one night just from the tips."

While prostitution is supposedly illegal in Burma, enforcement is often lax, like in many other societies in Asia. There is, of course, the bribe factor in play with police, but I could find no one willing to expound upon it.

Sadly, where education and opportunity seem to limit the draw of the sex industry in other regional countries, grinding poverty and low wages assures that it thrives here.

"The girls working in our shop include schoolgirls, nurses who are available to work at night, and university graduates," an unnamed source told AFP. "Many friends of mine work in [karaoke bars] or music pubs while also taking university correspondence courses," she said.

The idea is to escape. Get out of Burma and go somewhere where they can make something of themselves. Then help the family they left behind.

With an education this is possible in immigration terms, without one, though, the girls are simply hoping for a foreigner to rescue them. This is rare, however, and one could easily conclude that the girls are looking in all the wrong places for such an opportunity.

Living in Thailand, it is easy in Bangkok or Central Thailand to meet people who need to do visa runs to keep their immigration status legal. In the most basic terms, this requires an entry/exit stamp and a renewed visa. The border towns of Ranong, Thailand, and Kawthoung, Burma, located about 568 km south of Bangkok, provide this at a cost of less than THB3,000 (US$90).

Listening to stories from expats who have made this trip, it becomes obvious that some like to combine the chore of the visa run with a day of debauchery, dabbling in the local sex industry in Kawthoung.

"Last time I was down there I went exploring around Victoria Point on my own," explained one seasoned expat. "I came upon a small restaurant/karaoke bar and negotiated a price of about 12,000 kyats (US$10) for a short-time encounter for a nice, naive eighteen-year-old Burmese girl. The negotiation process, I must say, was no less interesting then the sex itself."

In Kawthoung the venues offering sexual services include karaoke bars, referred to as KTVs, which often double up as restaurants and bars. Though they have private rooms common to karaoke bars, in Kawthoung, at least, they seem to have decided against actually equipping these rooms with the TVs and music kits necessary for karaoke.

The expat continued.

"Setup of a Burmese karaoke in Kawthoung is that they don't call them karaoke bars, but just restaurants. Once you come in, a girl will bring you to one of [the] small rooms inside. You have to pay for 'one table' which includes a round of drinks, the table itself, and the girl's company. Then you have to pay for the girl separately, for any 'services' beyond just her company you would like her to provide. All together it still comes cheaper than most other Southeast Asia sex spots and you can enjoy cheap drinks during sex." He concluded with a brief look of nostalgia.

While the sex industry may seem to be struggling in third-world fashion in Kawthoung, bigger cities like the capital Rangoon see a much more bustling market. There, the KTVs actually have karaoke kits. There are also straight brothels, like in Kawthoung, but there is also the presence of freelance girls working in nightclubs and discos that doesn't exist elsewhere. In these clubs, sometimes housed in higher-end international hotels, the girls can outnumber the male clientele as much as ten to one, making competition fierce and driving down prices to be on a par with Kawthoung.

During a recent vacation that had a stopover in Kawthoung, I had the opportunity to experience Burma for myself. While I had no specific plan to explore the sex industry, an unlikely opportunity presented itself nonetheless.

I wandered around town taking in the sights and fighting off touts who were offering everything from pornographic VCDs, to Viagra, to prostitutes, to gay prostitutes, to more illicit drugs when the first offer was refused. They finally grew bored, or maybe frustrated, and moved on, leaving me on my own.

It was then that I happened upon what I can only assume to be one of the karaoke/restaurant bars I had heard about. Some half-dozen girls sat outside, smiling at me and calling out greetings, but were otherwise not too aggressive in attracting clients.

I went to a little "mama pop" store to restock on cigarettes, get a Coke, and various edible products. Thought nothing of it really, but the Burmese girl handling the transaction was quite beautiful: thin, long hair, statuesque, long legs, a pretty face with no make-up, and quite perky breasts for the average Asian girl. Yet I also wondered if she was actually eighteen. She looked young, maybe only fifteen or sixteen.

As she turned and went deeper into the store to fetch my Coke, I couldn't resist the opportunity to examine her backside. All of this attention on the shop girl caused me to overlook the elderly women fanning herself in the shadows.

She suddenly lunged forward from her seat, sensing and opportunity. "You want she?!" the woman asked. She wasn't an actual *mamasan,* more like simply Mama to the girl. I was shocked and caught off guard, and couldn't respond for a moment.

No matter, though, because Mama continued to push the hard sales pitch. "You want daughter? You take! Have hotel," she said pointing. "Fifteen dollar."

I stood for a moment, stunned. The shop girl had returned and was now standing next to her mother, shoulders slumped, head down, not daring to make eye contact. She obviously was not enjoying the prospect of being sold to someone for sex.

"No! Hell, no!" I exclaimed. While this may not have been an understandable rebuke for the mother, it was enough of a reaction for her to know that this was a no-sale situation. She scowled at me, probably figured I was a homosexual, and slunk back to her seat.

The shop girl never met my eyes after that as she completed our transaction, but I couldn't help but perceive a small smile on her face as her normal spirits returned. As I settled the bill and turned to leave, I heard her quietly say, "Thank you."

It is one of the very few experiences I have had in Asia where the girl on offer was certainly not willing to sell herself for sex; a sex slave with the front of a shop girl, being sold by her own mother. It was a sad situation that I won't soon forget and that will likely continue to play out until the country can rise above its status as an international pariah.

Frst published April 19, 2008 in *Asia Times Online*

A view on Vietnamese sex scandals

Actresses and models have been falling victim to scandals involving graphic nude photos and sex videos that are being distributed quickly across the Internet. While the young female burgeoning stars seem to always cry foul, many people are now beginning to wonder if some of these scandals are not publicity stunts.

Sex scandals are certainly nothing new, and the Internet has helped to fuel the easy, quick transfer of information. This insures that at the moment of release, there is no stopping the videos and images from spreading across the Web like wildfire as users copy, share, and re-post the material on servers around the world.

However, Asian Sex Gazette has learned that many are beginning to question the motives of the artists and models involved. In a developing story that is reminiscent of the "Pamela Anderson and Tommy Lee Sex Video", or the ongoing drama of the United States' newest media sex vixen, Paris Hilton, whose purportedly private sex videos have made her "Playboy's Sex Video Actress of the Year" for 2004, the Vietnamese are growing ever more suspicious of their young stars using sex in the media to capture fame.

In some cases, the "victims" have come forward to defend nude photography as art, while others have responded with general indifference. As a result, the public and authorities are now wondering if the "accidental" release of these materials onto the Internet may have been for the women seeking stardom to gain a greater share of the market.

Last year a sex video that an unknown Ho Chi Minh City dancing girl, known as HP, made with her ex-boyfriend propelled her to amateur stardom when the Vietnamese media gave it extensive coverage. As a result, Internet users in the country later voted the scandal as the "most terrific" media event of the year.

The short amateur video shows HP doing a sexy striptease for the camera, followed by the couple performing an array of hardcore sex acts with each other.

Paul Nguyen, president of Vietnam's top modeling agency Elite Models Vietnam, told local daily *Thanh Nien* that competition in the industry may be driving women's actions. "There are hundreds of models fighting for a job and the chance to be a top model," he said. "A top model with our agency can earn about US$12,000 a year after commissions."

While that may not seem like a lot of money, in Vietnam, where the average per capita income is US$483 per year according to the US State Department, US$12,000 is an extraordinary amount and offers a high standard of living.

So it seems that, given the rewards to be reaped, young women in the entertainment and modeling industries will consider an avenue that will allow them the opportunity to gain publicity. In order to gain attention as being more attractive and sexier than their competitors, some models, in certain cases, have even admitted to posting racy photos of themselves on the Internet.

Boa Hoa, one recent so-called victim, claimed that only privacy had been violated. Shooting nude photos is fine so long as they are kept private, she said of her nude photos that had appeared on the Internet. Local media seemed to side with Hoa, even though the photos were freely passed amongst agents, photographers, and clients in Vietnam with Hoa's knowledge. It was only once they made the Internet for public consumption that she became a victim in the eyes of the public and the media.

Compared to regional neighbors like Thailand, Vietnam has struggled to develop modeling as an industry. The modeling industry in Thailand has two main areas: mainstream models who shoot advertising photos for major brands, and these photos are then used throughout Southeast Asia, including Vietnam; and a grassroots but illegal pornography industry.

"The market is fragmented and small. Movie exposure helps for models but the movie industry in Vietnam is small, the models are underpaid for movie appearances, and the work takes a lot longer," said Paul Nguyen, whose agency manages more than twenty exclusive contract models and fifty to sixty other part-time and freelance models. He asserts that his agency does not produce any adult content.

"Vietnamese models have not yet really broken out into the international modeling scene," Nguyen said. "And foreign models often don't do well [or] are not paid enough in Vietnam." This leaves Vietnamese models fighting for whatever piece of the domestic modeling market they can get.

Another female personality and singer objected to racy, nude, and candid photos taken by an ex-lover; Nguyen Hong Nhung said that she would sue the ex for posting the photos on the Internet. Yet Nhung never prosecuted the matter officially, for reasons that remain unknown.

More recently is the "Yen Vy sex scandal", consisting of a pornographic film that is being distributed locally as copied video compact disk (VCD) on the black market and, of course, on the Internet. The actress and singer Yen Vy became the subject of sensational headlines, with many wondering if she was complicit in the release of the hardcore video.

Like any local porn scandal, it incites the moralists and conservatives to shout bloody murder over sex scenes that "devastate" the country's image and harm the youth. I personally disagree based upon the mantra that "any publicity is good publicity". Furthermore, upon seeing the Yen Vy video I decided that a trip to Vietnam might be in order, thus adding to the tourist boom that the video is creating.

Authorities are still struggling to figure out whether Vy had any knowledge about the production or release of the video, or whether she is just another victim. Here's a hint: Vy obviously knew where the camera was placed in terms of production at least.

Twenty-seven-year-old Vy has claimed to be a victim of blackmail, telling the media that an ex-lover filmed the tape five years ago during an affair that has since ended. Her lover apparently moved on after their relationship and married another woman, but the relationship fell apart. Destitute, the man contacted Vy, according to *Thanh Nien* (Youth) newspaper, but she refused his advances. As a result, according to Vy, he threatened to blackmail her with the thirty minute sex tape he had. Undeterred, Vy refused to give in, so he released the sex tape.

Police have since confirmed, according to local *Phap Luat* (Law) newspaper, that a formal complaint has been filed by Vy in what she characterizes as a hidden camera invasion of privacy, and release of intimate materials not meant for public consumption.

Meanwhile Vy, Hoa, HP, Nhung, and many others enjoy a flurry of local and international attention—in the blogosphere and local media anyway. The government and enforcement authorities seem impotent, or at least confused about taking action, as they cannot determine whether the women are victims or perpetrators in most cases.

Such a low level of enforcement does not satisfy some. Nguyen

The Thanh, deputy director of the HCM City Department of Culture and Information, argues that models and actresses should take responsibility for their actions.

"A number of artists or individuals like to expose their own naked bodies before the camera. That is their right, but when their privacy is exposed to the public, that is the price to pay. They have to pay the price for their choice of a way of living," *Nguoi Lao Dong* quoted Thanh as saying.

Thanh also commented that models and actresses have a responsibility to society to act morally, and that by not doing so has a negative impact on the public, especially the youth.

Exhibitionist tendencies are natural in some people, especially in terms of sexuality. As Vietnam experiences growing competition in its modeling and acting industries, it is not surprising that sex is becoming a forceful marketing tool.

The country still represses such tendencies by limiting sexual education and expression. But like many countries in the region, the women end up victims of human trafficking, are forced into prostitution via arranged marriages, or are led to believe that prostitution will help them provide for themselves and their families.

Even comely and beautiful Vietnamese models and actresses struggle, as this report demonstrates.

Sex will continue to be a taboo subject in Vietnam, as it is in many countries, but people will continue to exploit this taboo for personal gain.

Go ugly early

While many come to Asia seeking a tryst in the sex industry with a nubile young beauty of a sort they could never have enjoyed the company of in their home countries, there are some connoisseurs who operate under a far different methodology. These men believe there is far more value in taking a woman who is somewhat less than a beauty.

A close friend fell into this category, and explained his modus operandi as "go ugly early".

"Oh, it is great!" he exclaimed while swigging a beer. "You've never truly experienced the uninhibited joy of sex until you've taken an ugly bird."

He had a multitude of colorful explanations to justify his proclivity, many of which centered on why taking a beauty was more of a chore than a pleasure.

"You take a beautiful girl and that's all you get: a beautiful girl," he explained. "Half the time they just lie there figuring they look good and that is all they have to do. They don't get into it. Take an ugly girl or older woman, though, and it blows your mind—they seem to appreciate it, the attention. You get twice the action."

He continued his explanation, including details I suspect would have made Larry Flynt blush. Suffice to say, he felt that "less than pretty" women were more appreciative and thus more active sexually when getting male attention than the stunning beauties that just need to show up to draw men's affections.

My mates and I, of course, needled him over his proclivities,commenting that he was "out trolling for sea monsters" again, or, if he turned up late at the bar alone, whether the "big one got away" from him. He took it in good humor.

One night I stumbled upon him in a red-light district and found him chatting with a shocking specimen. A fine woman, no doubt, but time had not been kind to her. She was in her forties, I would guess, and sported thinning hair, sagging breasts, and an unfortunate set of teeth that seemed to point in more directions than a compass was capable of.

"I see you have found your sea monster for the evening," I said in an aside to him.

"Who? Her?" he asked, reaching out and groping her playfully. "Oh no, she is far too beautiful for me."

I shuddered. "You're joking!"

"He's not," a mutual friend chimed in, who happened to be his roommate. "I get to wake up to the carnage. Sober and hung over, it is not a pretty sight."

"Well, you can keep your sea monsters," I told him. "I will stick to the pretty girls."

"You're missing out," he responded, "but more for me then, I guess."

Months later I met another fellow drinking at a bar in Pattaya, Thailand, with whom I shared this line of thought to get his opinion on the subject.

"Your mate has got it spot on!" he exclaimed over the booming music. "I couldn't have explained it better myself."

I shook my head in slight fascination.

"A few weeks ago I was up on Soi Cowboy in some go-go bar," he continued, referring to an area in Bangkok famous for its entertainment venues. "Plenty of beautiful women dancing around half-naked, but I spotted this waitress. She was fat, positively rotund, I swear a hundred kilos if she was a gram. Bought her a few drinks and before I know it she is telling me that if I pay her barfine and give her THB1,000 (US$30), she'll go with me all night. That's like half the price those other girls would have charged just for short time," he said, obviously pleased with himself.

He drained his beer, and then continued: "I get her back to the hotel and this girl is all over me, not shy at all. At one point she has got me in a '69' position with her on top; I swear I thought I was going to suffocate, saw my life flash before my eyes and everything. Marvelous, bloody marvelous!"

I interrupted his roaring laughter by asking him, "You remember the bar, or the girl's name?" For I had now realized what had gained my interest about his story: there are not many girls on Soi Cowboy who fit this description.

"No, I don't really remember, why?" he asked.

"You think it might have been Tilac Bar?" I inquired.

"Actually, yeah, I think it was," he replied, now a bit taken aback.

"Was her name Duen?" I asked with a wry smile.

"Holy shit!" he said, choking on his beer. "How did you know that? Have you taken her before?"

"Oh no," I answered. "Never taken Duen, I will leave her to you. She's a friend, that's all."

A few days later back in Bangkok, I couldn't resist the urge of stopping by Tilac Bar to see Duen. Seeing me enter the somewhat crowded bar, she got my usual drink without needing to be asked. She then sat down with me and we went through the usual small talk, exchanging pleasantries. After a while she asked the inevitable question as to where my wife Noi was. I assured her that Noi was fine, just not out tonight (they had become friends too).

I offered to buy Duen a lady drink, which she happily accepted.

I finally broached the subject of the *farang* customer of hers I had met, adding that he seemed to have enjoyed her company very much. She looked confused for a few moments, so I added, "His name is Michael, he's British." Still nothing, so I added, against my better judgment, "Said you damned near killed him in the '69' position!"

That did it. She broke into a wide smile and said, "Yes, Michael, I remember him. He was nice. We have good time! Do you think he will come back and see me again soon?" Obviously, she hoped he would.

"I would say there is a very strong chance that he will," I replied honestly.

As I had learned, for some men there was simply no competition to a woman like Duen.

By the numbers: consensual sex in Asia

Societies all over the world struggle to legally and morally define the age that young people can consent to sex, and it is an issue complicated by religion, sexually conservative and opportunistic politicians, and moralists. In Asia the laws defining the ages of consent are as varied and complex as those found in the West.

When considering age of sexual consent, there are three categories that are usually defined: male and female sex, regarded as vaginal penetrative sex; male on male homosexual sex, thought of as anal penetrative sex; and female lesbian sex, which apparently lacks definition of what gets penetrated.

In most Muslim countries, though, there is no need to put forth a specific age of consent for homosexual relationships because they are illegal anyway. In the extreme, countries such as Afghanistan, Iran, Pakistan, and Saudi Arabia can punish homosexual behavior, at least amongst males, with death. In addition, the age of consent for a male and female sexual relationship is not defined at all, so long as the couple meet the requirement of being married.

In these Muslim countries and others, this often means that consent is based simply upon marriage and not age, thus spouses of either sex can be quite young, although it is usually the women and girls in these relationships that end up being the younger ones. Sadly, media reports seem to indicate that girls are sometimes married off as young as six years old.

The "must be married" without specification of age to consent to sex applies in Iran, Kuwait, Pakistan, Saudi Arabia, and Yemen, while Afghanistan, Bahrain, Lebanon, Malaysia, and the United Arab Emirates do specify an age—ranging from fifteen to eighteen years old—and only between married couples, yet these age requirements can often be ignored in some of these countries.

The requirement of marriage can also be largely ignored in many of these countries when it comes to prostitution or casual relationships, but the punishment—which can be quite severe and include death—is usually faced by the female rather than the male. This is similar to adultery cases in many of these countries.

Then there are countries like Japan and the Philippines that have the lowest ages of consent in the world at just twelve years old (shared only with Angola, Mexico, and Zimbabwe). Granted that, in terms of Japan, the law allowing consent at age twelve only applies in metro Tokyo, it cannot be applied in a situation of prostitution or used by an older man in a position of authority. Japan's federal laws rule sexual consent in Japan to be thirteen years of age, but prefecture law usually can and does override federal law, raising the age up to eighteen. However, this is usually only applied to prosecute cases of prostitution, sexual abuse, or the abuse of authority by older men who coerce sex from women under eighteen.

Similarly, in the Philippines the age of sexual consent is twelve for both males and females. But sexual intercourse with a minor (a person under eighteen) is an offense if, like in Japan, the minor's consent is based upon prostitution or coercion. For these reasons, both the Philippines and Japan fall into a sort of "twelve to eighteen" category to define the age of sexual consent, depending on the nature of the sexual relationship.

Similarly, the popular sex tourist destination of Thailand has an age of sexual consent of fifteen, but this seems to apply only to locals and in the sex industry, sex with a girl of fifteen is illegal; girls working the trade must be eighteen or older.

Meanwhile, South Korea gets the nod as the runner-up for the country with the youngest age of sexual consent in Asia. Homosexual or not, the age is just thirteen. South Korea is followed by China, Brunei, Israel, Mongolia, and India, which allow sex at fourteen years old, at least in the heterosexual category.

Then there are the half dozen countries consisting of Burma, Malaysia, Singapore, Sri Lanka, Tajikistan, Turkmenistan, and Uzbekistan that seem to have the almost humorous laws of making homosexual sex between males illegal, while at the same time specifically defining the age of lesbian sexual consent to be sixteen. One has to wonder if, while considering legislation concerning the age of consent in these countries, the lawmakers said, "Male homosexual sex, that's unnatural," then in the next breath pondered, "Lesbian sex, now that's hot."

The average age for sexual consent across all categories in Asia is between fourteen and fifteen years old, an average based upon the countries that specify an age (14.75 for male/female sex; 13.8 for male/male sex; and 14.5 for female/female sex). This figure is not far from the average in the West, such as the US where the average state law age of sexual consent is sixteen years old.

However, US federal law strictly adheres to the premise that an adult is defined as someone eighteen years or older, making anyone seventeen or under a minor. Recent federal legislation has also sought to criminalize sex tourism with underage persons abroad. If a US citizen has sex with a minor abroad, the minor comes under the federal definition of a minor, regardless of whether the act was legal in the country's in which the act was performed. The PROTECT Act of 2003 will prosecute Americans for having sex with women under the age of eighteen while traveling overseas.

Conveniently for American authorities, it seems that almost all trans-Pacific flights from East Asia land in California, a location where even the state law defines the age of sexual consent for all types of sex, by the definitions described herein, to be a minimum of eighteen years old.

Similar laws have recently been passed in Canada, some European countries, and, most notably, Britain and Australia. Back in Asia many countries like Korea, Japan, Indonesia, Thailand, and Cambodia have increased the diplomatic exchange of information in the form of providing lists of known pedophiles, locally arresting Westerns caught having sex with underage persons while traveling, or by being increasingly cooperative in extraditing a guilty foreigner back to their home country. Whether or not the traveler faces prosecution under local laws, they will often face the justice system back in their home country.

Questions surrounding such matters were brought to a head recently when an American journalist trolling the bars of Hong Kong's red-light district of Wan Chai happened upon a "roaming *mamasan*" who hopped from bar to bar looking for customers for her girls. She approached the journalist seated alone and asked him if he wanted a girl better than the ones that particular bar had to offer. He was confused as he had never been approached in this manner before. Nevertheless, he was intrigued and let her continue her sales pitch. She claimed to have a half dozen or so girls in her charge nearby: beautiful, young, cute—and Chinese.

He agreed, telling her that was exactly what he wanted: a young, cute, beautiful Chinese girl. A phone call or two later and she returned, confident that she had the perfect girl for him. She told him that a better place to meet would be Joe Banana's on nearby Jaffe Road, a pub/restaurant rather than a freelance pick-up bar.

She assured him that the girl would know him when she arrived as she had described him to her. He just had to make sure that he sat alone. Any problems and the girl would call the *mamasan* on her mobile phone. The price was HK$1,500 (US$190) for as long as he wanted, short time or all night.

When the girl arrived, she made her way to his table and was everything that the *mamasan* had promised: cute yet beautiful, sexy, short and petite, with long hair and porcelain white skin that seemed flawless. Her English was almost non-existent, but the two of them managed to communicate, and he was intrigued to learn that she was, in fact, a Chinese mainlander.

That night back at this apartment he was amazed by her enthusiasm and seemingly unquenchable thirst for sex; he lost count of the number of times they had sex, let alone the playful manual and oral stimulation they shared with each other.

Unsurprisingly, he really liked the girl and only a week or so later called her again to arrange for her company. This time she came straight to his apartment and wasted no time, tossing her purse on the side table, ripping his T-shirt off and throwing it aside, then doing the same with her own. Soon they were naked amongst a pile of clothes. She pushed him back and mounted him, holding him firmly as she rode him to climax. She left him panting and sweaty on the couch as she made for the bathroom.

While she was away, he finally began to take in the room around him, and noticed her spilled purse on the table beside him. In particular, he noticed her Hong Kong Identification Card. Picking it up and studying it for a moment, he started doing the basic math and realized suddenly that she was seventeen years old, a few months short of her eighteenth birthday.

He was aghast. Being American, he knew there was a possibility of this being viewed quite differently in his homeland. Even though Hong Kong's local law puts the age of sexual consent at sixteen, the manner in which they had conducted their business-based rendezvous, namely through prostitution, was illegal. Any local prosecution or local record of the events would be damning, as any account would then be passed to US authorities and prosecuted by the American justice system, which would label him as a pedophile.

The American ended their relationship after that night, but his experience is hardly unique. Girls of all ages ply the sex trade and don't go out of their way to reveal their true ages. Foreigners seeking underage sex is one thing, but falling into the situation accidentally is quite another entirely, and one that is not to be taken lightly.

These laws put forth by societies are intended to protect youths from exploitation and abuse. Yet all too often these same laws are circumvented, ignored, or not enforced. Women's rights are an issue in this realm too, as the laws so often seem to favor the male and put the onus on the female's behavior.

In some regards, lack of enforcement within Asian societies can surprisingly, in some cases, be more logical. An eighteen year old with a consenting fourteen year old is acceptable in most of Asia; a twenty-six year old having consensual sex with a seventeen year old is also not a problem; a forty-five year old having consensual sex with a seventeen year old is generally acceptable in Asia so long as the exacerbating factors of prostitution, abuse, or coercion are not present.

A lack of enforcement in Asia can sometimes be positive, in a very limited sense, and only because the contrast highlights the failures in Western societies: where the US would prosecute an eighteen year old for having sex with his long-term sixteen-year-old girlfriend, most Asian countries would never consider such a thing.

The US is currently wielding the ultra-conservative view that youth sex is unacceptable, and globally pushing this view financially by only supporting efforts that advocate abstinence. Aside from Muslim nations, Asia seems to take a somewhat more enlightened and certainly more liberal approach to youth sexuality. The sort of "sliding scale" approach Asia applies to sex and age, so long as there are no aggravating factors in the relationship, seems more logical than the attitude of Western nations, which create strict definitions and enforce them vigorously and, sometimes, absurdly.

Puberty usually happens during teenaged years, bringing with it curiosity, waves of hormones, and a desire to explore sexuality. While politicians, religious leaders, and parents want to preserve the youth and innocence of their "children", the fact remains that these children have now become young adults. Trying to suppress sexuality among young adults throughout the world through legislation, strict laws, or abstinence-only education is akin to screaming with rage at the skies in an attempt to stop the rain.

The land of the Karma Sutra flunks sex ed

Home of the Karma Sutra, a press that screams about sex every chance it gets, and a population of well over 1 billion, India is a country where sex pervades many aspects of daily life. Yet as recent reports show, it struggles to come to terms with sexuality as educators, parents, and politicians squabble over sex education.

This week the Ministry of Education in Maharashtra State, Central India, announced that it was planning to reintroduce sex education to schools. The move comes a year after protests by parents and politicians prompted the Ministry of Education to pull its existing curriculum because it was deemed "too graphic".

Apparently, black-and-white cartoon-style cross-sections of a penis or a vagina are too graphic. In a country that struggles with sexually transmitted diseases, HIV/AIDS, unplanned parenthood, an exploding population, and gender-selective abortions, one might think sex education would be something of a priority.

Unfortunately, it isn't. In fact, sex education is banned in many Indian states, a fact that's increasingly frustrating to educators. "If somebody's life [could be] ruined by lack of scientific knowledge, it's the state's responsibility to provide it," Vasant Purke, education minister of Maharashtra, told media this week.

Throughout India young people are presented with sexual

content in magazines, newspapers, movies, and on television and the Internet. As someone who monitors sex news, I'm amazed how often I receive news alerts from major Indian daily news sources. But as for stories about sex in India, there's nothing at all.

The news alerts from Indian sources are almost always a sex story from the West that the Indian media have picked up. They run with sensational headlines like "Paris Hilton sex tape released!" or "American Idol contestant Antonella Barba nude pictures surface!" Not to mention, for the tenth time, "Paparazzi photograph catches Britney Spears without panties!" The screaming headlines inevitably conclude with the old "dog's dick", as exclamation marks are sometimes called in the print media.

It's tiresome stuff. Even Americans have grown bored of such celebrity antics, so one has to wonder why the average Indian would be interested in this softcore smut.

The truth is they're not. Although Indians might look up the pictures on the Internet, many couldn't care less about Britney, Paris, and so on, if they even know who they are. The fact is Indians are interested in the sex angle of the so-called stories. The sex angle, at least in its salacious and entertaining aspect, is never mentioned in local Indian news reports. In fact, other than "bad news" in the form of scandals, sex education woes, sex crimes, or prostitution busts, the Indian media almost entirely shies away from reporting on sex.

Considering that India gave the world the Karma Sutra— possibly the first illustrated how-to manual for intercourse ever written—in the second century, India may have been one of the earliest countries in Asia to have had a sexual revolution. In international terms, the Greeks were first in the field, of course, but other than its open society towards sex, the Greeks have accomplished little since, unless you count an affinity for anal sex and switch-hitting bi-sexuality.

Getting back to sex ed: it's clear the Karma Sutra shouldn't be used as an educational tool for young students, but basic educational materials shouldn't be excluded. After all, it's an erotic guide meant to heighten the pleasure of the sexual act. However, in the country that produced it one might expect a little more tolerance in terms of talking openly about sex. It wasn't until 1972 that *The Joy of Sex* came out in America, a time when the US was gripped by its own sexual revolution. The US, which is considered downright prudish by European standards, has mandatory sex ed in public schools and doesn't seem to have a huge problem with those cartoon penises and vagina drawings found in sexual education schoolbooks.

Seriously, consider the following scenario: A teacher steps before a classroom of teenagers and says, "You may have noticed half of you have one of these" while raising a cartoon drawing of the penis. The teacher then lifts the drawing of a vagina and adds, "The other half of you have one of these."

Continuing this hypothetical lesson, the teacher then explains that, in time, the students might discover the desire to have these two physical interfaces interact. There are a myriad of reasons for this, the teacher continues, for example, love, hormones, or peer pressure. Ultimately, though, the blushing teacher gets around to the fact that such interaction—sex, obviously—can result in unwanted pregnancy or worse, a life-threatening disease. The potential consequences of sex seem enough to sway everyone to advocate open talk and government-sanctioned sex education.

But in India, even simple lessons and straight talk about sex are non-existent. On April 23 ministers of Maharashtra's state government lashed out at the Ministry of Education and Minister Purke, characterizing his announcement to reinstate sex ed as rouge and brash.

Shobha Phadanvis, a female member of India's opposition

Bharatiya Janata Party, even absurdly warned that introducing such a curriculum without careful study could lead to an increase in teachers who sexually abuse students, another controversial issue in India's schools. How does that work exactly? "Alright, girls, take out your notebook, pencil and show me your vagina!"

At least if girls had received sex education they would know that they were being "sexually" abused.

State Assembly speaker Babasaheb Kupekar tabled the sex ed proposal indefinitely on April 23, citing the need for further consultation from experts and academics. Meanwhile, another BJP member, Mangalprabhat Lodha, called the proposal "ignorant" and charged that it did not take into consideration the cultural, moral, and societal factors of the people in the state.

True enough, this controversy contains a profound amount of ignorance. The sex classes are aimed at educating students in the ninth and eleventh years of education, when they would be typically fourteen and seventeen years old. Logic suggests that at that age, many would've figured out a few things for themselves.

In the Western country where I was raised, sex education was a minor part of the curriculum from the first grade—about seven or eight years old—and it came up as a topic each year thereafter. It was nothing shocking: those penis and vagina cartoons were on hand and I learned where babies come from.

But parents in India are woefully conservative in terms of sex. As such, they're unlikely to have "The Talk" with their children. Sadly, it seems children are left to their own devices to learn about sexuality. It's almost enough to make you appreciate that the global pornography network—a.k.a the Internet—exists. Hey, at least young people can find information there while their parents squabble about "controversial" issues. Here's a message for India to mull over: damning your children to unwanted pregnancy, diseases, and overall negative sexual experiences is not a great way to manage your society.

First published April 26, 2008 in *Asia Times Online*

Grrl power Asia:
hear it growl

The modern feminist movement faces many challenges. As a product of Western civilization, it is probably little surprise that Eastern cultures don't seem to measure up in terms of women's rights, which can sometimes be deplorable in Asia. For all the dissatisfaction that their feminist "sisters" in the West may feel for their Asian sisters, it might not always be what they think.

Asian women are viewed as demure and subservient when compared to their Western counterparts, and in many cases this is categorically true. Yet the fact that many women in Asian cultures are not complaining, protesting, or declaring war on the male species, seems to be overlooked.

Certainly some South Asian or Middle Eastern countries struggle significantly with women's rights, often due to religious and societal limitations. For example, the deplorable idea of honor killings must be stopped, and I hope that through education, human rights initiatives, and tolerance that it will be eradicated, hopefully in this generation.

Some societies also impose harsh penalties on women who commit "infidelity" (sometimes all the woman has done is sit in the company of an unrelated male). Punishment can range from lashings to death by stoning. These are stunning examples of the lack of women's—and human—rights that everyone should have access to. The West is fighting Islamic fundamentalism, spending billions of dollars fighting terrorism. Yet it is only the underfunded NGOs and human rights organizations that step up to defend women.

If there was ever a place where human (women's) rights need to be addressed, it is Asia (Africa too, but I write on Asia, sorry). However, whilst Asian women can be demure and seemingly subservient, some are anything but.

While dating an affluent Shanghai girl, I was stunned when she laid out to me in detail our future: I would be going back to school to get my law degree, I would get a job at a good law firm, and that this would help me to support the family and babies we'd be having. This didn't seem negotiable, but I was silently negotiating my exit.

In Japan, Korea, and China, women often hold a very strong and vocal position. While feminist purists would still find this unacceptable, the women in these cultures hold these positions in high regard. A wife will often push her husband towards success, and not be shy about admonishing him if he failed to fulfill his role to support the family adequately.

In addition, women in those East Asian countries are increasing becoming upwardly mobile in an expanding middle class. Many are being offered, and seizing, more and more opportunities, increasingly becoming successful and independent in many areas of business and government.

Certainly there is always room for improvement, but things seem to be moving in the right direction. However, the more rabid feminists could still easily find plenty of examples to support their arguments that these same countries are still in the in the dark ages in terms of women's rights, and to some extent they may be right.

Arguing that feminism is somehow being restrained by a

male stranglehold on the metaphorical leash that holds women back, as is sometimes claimed in the West, would be wrong too. In many of these societies, Asian women themselves seem to lack the motivation to push the issue much.

Ui, a young middle-class office worker employed as an administrative assistant in Southeast Asia says, "In my opinion, feminism is a positive influence in modern society. At present women can do everything [the] same as men, women can work and do everything by themselves these days. Maybe women can do it better than men in some cases. We don't want the men to take advantage [of] us, so in that aspect we want feminism to help us in society when issues arise."

When asked about feminist protests on campuses in the West, where protesters sometimes chant anti-male rhetoric with signage about male oppression, only to be met by male students seeking to incite them with signs like "Iron my shirt, bitch", she was less supportive. She said that she felt such actions in much of Asia would upset social order and harmony.

In this regard, it would seem that Asian feminists have taken a more delicate approach to feminism that includes recognition for the religious and social roles women play in society. While they are not discounting the actions of their Western sisters, they are not willing—and not for negative reasons, usually—to challenge societal roles. To "centralist" women, or people, in the women's rights movement this would seem acceptable, maybe even deserving commendation.

Sitting in a local bar one evening this week, I decided to ask what the girls working at the bar thought of feminism. After some confusion as I tried to translate this concept for them, I ultimately settled on the description that men and women are the same.

Joom, a confused look on her face, said, "But men and women

are not same, men have a [penis] and women ..."

"No, no, that is not what I mean," I said as her friend Sorn nodded her head in profound agreement with Joom, both looking rather worried that I had failed a health class or had fallen prey to only ladyboys thus far. This was finally cleared up when I explained the idea of women's rights, where women are treated as equals and not as sex objects.

This was met with stunned silence. "But women are sexy and they want to be, most [of] the time," Sorn argued.

I tried to explain the idea that women should not be viewed solely on their sexiness, and that men should not treat them.

Joom, who looked a bit intrigued, said, "But you said as 'equals' women are meant to be sexy. Men come to the bar that are rich, see me, and think I am sexy. Then I am equal, because suddenly this 'big man' becomes a little boy. I can make him [part with his] money for a few minutes of pleasure." She added, "I am more powerful then. If I wasn't sexy, I would not have that power."

During a brief discussion I tried to tell them that feminists in the West would see them as being exploited for sex, dolling themselves up in make-up to look sexy for men and stuck in societal roles forced on them by gender: prostitute, housewife, or at the very least, being more limited in their choice of jobs and earnings than men are.

Sorn was unmoved. "Women are meant to have babies and raise them. That mean we will take care of the home. I don't want a big [high paying] job, I want to meet a good man to be my husband, take care of me, have children and I will take care of him."

Joom seemed to agree but her mind was elsewhere, asking, "Do women in your country—these 'feminists'—actually do what you are saying? Get angry for men looking at sexy women?

[Adopt butch styles] Cutting their hair, not wear make-up and dress like men?"

In answering, I tried to be careful to point out that it is only a few, but that many women hold views that include some facets of what we had discussed.

To this Joom replied, "No wonder [foreigners] like Asia so much."

Joom may be right in this regard. Men have expressed many times in their own way that it is nice to be somewhere that they can tell a woman that she is beautiful or sexy and have it be taken as a compliment rather than resulting in a lawsuit.

To say that women anywhere in Asia are "against" feminism would be categorically wrong; they support it, yearn for it, and hope that the future will bring about positive change. The difference is that they do not take such a hard line about it as feminists do in the West.

We should all find ways to support women's rights. If not under the header of "feminist", then at least by supporting human rights and those of women. By speaking out, advocating, reporting, and offering support to organizations like The Global Fund for Women and Human Rights Watch, we can hope to bring about the change that is so often lacking, but that women have long deserved.

Later, back at the bar when I was paying my bill, Joom came over with a quizzical look and inquired, "This equal thing you talked about, would that mean that men would have to [perform oral sex] every time too?"

I giggled as I shook my head. "I don't know, Joom, maybe, I guess."

This was met with a beaming smile from her. It wasn't until I was half way home that I realized I might have just helped indoctrinate another young woman into the modern feminist movement—but I doubt I will be earning any points with feminists based on her motives.

First published May 3, 2008 in *Asia Times Online*

Sex in the Chinese city

The young women in the cosmopolitan and Western-influenced Special Administrative Region of modern Hong Kong have views on sex and relationships akin to those of their Western counterparts. Sexual freedom, expression, and experimentation are blooming, while in Greater China women, though in the midst of a sexual revolution, still often struggle with traditional roles. I was given the unique opportunity to join the girls for a night out and gain insight into the modern Chinese women of Hong Kong.

In a local Western-chain bar and restaurant near my home in Hong Kong that I frequented after work for a drink and sometimes dinner, I became friends with the few *gweilo* and the mainly local Chinese staff. One young woman in particular, twenty-two-year-old Fiona, was especially nice and liked to converse with me on a range of topics. One of her favorite subjects was the triumphs or unjust defeats of her favorite football club, Arsenal.

Being an American, this was a little harder for me to follow, but working for a local paper, I found myself at least checking the sports news and league standings, so I was able to nod in agreement of sigh in resignation at the right moments during our chats about Arsenal. Ultimately, we became friends and I was surprised when she invited me to join her and her friends on their night off—a night that was effectively a "girls' night out".

I quickly accepted as I wanted to see what a girls' night out consisted of by Hong Kong Chinese standards.

I found myself waiting at the busy but efficient Tsim Sha Tsui station and, as directed by Fiona, was lingering near exit B. I stood watching the endless crush of passengers either making their way home from work, heading to another evening appointment, or simply waiting idly, as I was, out of the stream of foot traffic. I could not help but notice a beautiful young Chinese girl waiting on the other side of the sea of people passing by.

I noticed her because she was beautiful; but then I became intrigued because she seemed to have noticed me too. Maybe she was reacting to my glances, maybe she thought I was some sex-starved sexual predator, or could she think, I thought bemused, that I was attractive?

At least the sexual-predator scenario was discounted moments later when she gave me a brief, ambiguous smile before turning her attention elsewhere.

Fiona and her friend finally arrived, dressed up to the nines; at work Fiona was forced to wear the somewhat dull Western uniform of her franchise employer, and the employer obviously didn't recognize the value of letting the girls dress themselves. Fiona looked great. She failed to notice me straight away and instead, with her female Chinese friend in tow, headed straight for the beautiful young woman I had been sharing glances with.

After a brief interlude, Fiona looked in my direction, obviously informed by the girl that there was a waiting *gweilo* watching them. My heart skipped a bit. I wasn't the sexual predator, nor the horny *gweilo*, but rather the person Fiona had told her that they would be meeting. They all crossed over to me in a kind, reassuring, and jovial manner.

Fiona introduced everyone; the beauty in waiting was named Stephanie and Fiona's companion was Shirley. I flushed as I shook hands with Stephanie, worried that surely she'd seen it, and then shook hands with the others as well.

We made our way to a Kashmiri-inspired Indian restaurant—

which served a lovely chicken tikka masala, as it turned out—to eat, drink, and talk.

All three of the women had boyfriends to some degree. Fiona was in committed relationship, Stephanie was in a bit of a transient one, and Shirley was more exploratory and dating various men.

Dinner was spicy and delicious, and the conversations were similar.

"My mom has her 'boy toy' after divorcing my dad. It is bullshit," Fiona complained. "I meet this boyfriend of hers and he is closer to my age group than to my mom's."

Stephanie chimed in. "I know what you mean, I met my dad's latest girlfriend and she is only a few years older than me. It's weird. He told me to treat her as a sister. He obviously didn't realize that this just made it more awkward. I mean, if she was my sister that just makes it sick!"

"I kind of expect that from men," Fiona said, glancing suspiciously at me, wondering what my reaction might be. "But with my mom and her boyfriend it is even worse. I mean, as a woman anytime you meet a man about your age you just kind of naturally size them up in terms of sex, but doing that with your mom's boyfriend, now that's awkward!"

The women all laughed and agreed. This last part wasn't lost on me, though, as were none of the quick glances in my direction from each of the girls. I shuffled my feet under the table as I wondered to myself how exactly I had measured up when they'd each met me.

Stephanie smiled coyly as she seemed to understand what I was thinking. Wine flowed and the conversation continued. At times the girls switched to Chinese as the subject grew spirited, but Stephanie, who was sitting across from me, or Fiona always made sure they'd give me the basic gist in English.

Shirley related a story about a previous short-lived relationship with a local man who apparently didn't measure up in a particular physical sense, which drew laughs from the other girls. Then Stephanie made a comment saying she didn't date Chinese men that often and that maybe Western men did have their advantages. Another winning smile headed in my direction. I had effectively been objectified, and I didn't mind at all.

Fiona worked in the bar that I frequented, and much to my pleasure I learned that Stephanie had just been hired to work there too. Fiona was in a long-term relationship with her Chinese boyfriend and seemed happy, though she didn't know where the relationship would lead.

Stephanie, it turned out, was a nineteen-year-old (I suppressed a shudder) American-born Chinese (ABC) college girl taking the summer off. She'd come to Hong Kong to visit her mother. Leaving behind an American boyfriend, she wondered where that relationship would go as she was planning to continue her studies that fall in Europe.

On the other hand, Shirley was single and fancy free. She also traveled a lot for her job and was happy to meet new men on her journeys. She was sure that one day she would stumble upon Mr Right.

Dinner drew to a close and we spilled out onto the busy streets of Hong Kong. Shirley and Fiona were chatting animatedly in Chinese, apparently deciding where to go next. Stephanie turned to me and said that where they were going was a Chinese-style karaoke and pick-up joint, and that I probably wouldn't enjoy it.

I am sure I looked disappointed as I felt myself deflate, but a moment later she responded by saying that we could go someplace and get a drink together instead, as she wasn't really interested in karaoke bars. If I had been deflated seconds earlier, her suggestion certainly picked me up.

We said goodbye to Fiona and Shirley, who made off on foot to the Chinese bars of Tsim Sha Tsui. Stephanie and I took the train to the trendy Lan Kwai Fong yuppie party district. We settled on Fong Bar, where a male friend of hers worked as a bartender. He regarding me with curiosity, probably wondering where Stephanie had found the *gweilo*, but he was friendly when we were introduced.

Stephanie and I chose a table located in a corner where it was a little quieter and we could talk privately. We talked about various relationships we were in or had been in. My wife was in Thailand, Stephanie's boyfriend back in San Francisco.

"Why doesn't she stay with you here in Hong Kong?" she asked.

"She doesn't like Hong Kong," I said, adding, "it's not easy for her to find food that she likes, misses her friends, and it is hard for her to make new friends here." I thought to myself but didn't admit to her that I knew we had been growing apart for a while.

"You must get lonely here in Hong Kong by yourself then," she said seriously, as if she worried about me. It made my personal longing deeper and I think she sensed it.

"Yeah, I guess, of course," I answered, looking blankly into space. I changed the subject. "What about you? You miss your boyfriend back in the States?"

She sighed before answering. "I do, yes, but, I don't know, we are still so young. It is not like it is anything so serious and like I said, I will be leaving to finish my education in Europe this fall. This sort of relationship, at our age, doesn't survive a long-distance separation."

We talked for a few hours before calling it a night and heading home. I was intrigued by this young woman who was so worldly at such an early age, anchored in reality, independent, and, of course, beautiful.

Sometime later, sitting at the bar talking to Fiona as she worked, we both watched Stephanie as she collected some drinks, flashed a warm, happy smile to us both, then turned and walked off to deliver the drinks to one of the tables.

Out of nowhere, Fiona asked me, "You guys had sex that night we all went out, right?"

I choked on my drink and sputtered, "No!"

"Huh?" she said. She broke from my gaze, and looked at Stephanie moving between tables. "You guys really seemed to connect."

When I spoke with Stephanie, I told her what Fiona had said and she blushed. I promptly told her that I had replied no to the question, then reflexively added, "I wish!"

Stephanie smiled one of her warm smiles, blushed a bit more, and answered only with a giggle.

In Pakistan, a dark trade comes to light

In the Islamic nation of Pakistan, prostitution, once relegated to dark alleys and small red-light districts, is now seeping into many neighborhoods of the country's urban centers. Reports indicate that since the end of civilian rule in 1977, times have changed and now the sex industry is bustling.

Early military governments and religious groups sought to reform areas like the famous "Taxali Gate" district of Lahore by displacing prostitutes and their families in an effort to "reinvent" the neighborhood.

While displacing the prostitutes might have temporarily made the once small red-light district a better neighborhood for a time, it did little to stop the now dispersed prostitutes from plying their trade. Reforming a neighborhood, instead of offering education and alternative opportunities, appears to be at the core of early failures to curb the nascent sex industry. This mistake has become a prophetic error, as now the tendrils of the sex trade have become omnipresent in cities like Islamabad, Rawalpindi, Karachi, and Lahore, not to mention towns, villages, and rural outposts.

An aid worker for an Islamabad-based NGO recently related a story: Soon after his arrival in the capital, he realized the house next to his own was a Chinese brothel. The Chinese ability to "franchise" the commercial sex industry by providing downtrodden Chinese women throughout Asia, North America, and Europe would be admirable in a business sense if it were not for the atrocities—human trafficking, sexual slavery, and exploitation—which cloud its practice.

Chinese bordellos, often operating as massage parlors or beauty salons, can be found across Pakistan, and have even spread to war-torn and restive locations such as the Afghan capital Kabul. When it comes to the sex industry, the Chinese have developed a cunning ability to recognize areas where the demand for sex far outstrips the supply.

The NGO worker said that after months of living adjacent to the brothel, things were shaken up—literally. One evening a drunken Pakistani drove his car into the brothel. Later the driver told authorities the ramming was a protest by a devout Muslim against the debauchery taking place in the house by its inhabitants. The NGO worker, however, had seen the same car parked peacefully outside the house the night before and wondered if instead the local man might not actually be a disgruntled customer who hadn't got the "happy ending" he had hoped for.

The local sex industry, comprising of Pakistani prostitutes, has also grown in recent years. One can easily find videos on YouTube that show unabashed red-light areas of Lahore. The videos display house after house with colorfully lit entrances, always with a *mamasan* and at least one Pakistani woman in traditional dress. The women are available for in-house services for as little as 400 rupees (US$6), with take-away prices ranging from 1,000 rupees (US$14) to 2,000 rupees (US$28). These districts are mostly for locals, but foreigners can indulge at higher prices.

Foreigners in Pakistan have no trouble finding companionship and may receive rates similar to locals in downtrodden districts. More upscale areas like Lahore's Heera Mundi, or "Diamond Market", cater to well-heeled locals and foreigners. At these places prettier, younger girls push their services for between 5,000 rupees (US$70) and 10,000 rupees (US$140) for an all-night visit. The most exceptional can command between 20,000 (US$280) and 40,000 rupees (US$555) for just short time.

Rumors abound online that female TV stars and actresses can be hired for sex. "You can get film stars for 50,000 (US$695) to 100,000 rupees (US$1,400) but you need good contacts for that," one blogger wrote after a trip to Lahore.

"The Lahore, Karachi, and Rawalpindi sex scenes are totally changing and it's easier and easier to get a girl for [sex]," another blogger wrote. "Most of the hotels provide you the girls upon request." Bloggers also reported that it is easy to find girls prowling the streets after 6 pm, and foreigners can find young women hanging out near Western franchises like McDonald's and KFC. Such women, the bloggers claim, can lead the customer to nearby short-time accommodation.

Short-time hotels offering hourly rates can be found all over major cities, underscoring the profits being reaped by the sex industry.

Pakistan can also accommodate the gay community with prostitution. Unfortunately, this has also given rise to child prostitution.

A Pakistani blogger wrote, "We [ethnic] Pathans are very fond of boys. [In Pakistan] the wives are only [had sex with] once or twice a year. There are a lot of gay brothels in Peshawar—the famous among them is at Ramdas Bazaar. [One can] go to any Afghan restaurant and find young waiters selling sex."

As in many societies, access to technology, the Internet, and mobile phones has only facilitated the sex trade in Pakistan. Matchmaking websites serve the male clientele, while providing marketing for prostitutes.

The root causes of prostitution in Pakistan are poverty and a dearth of opportunities. Widows find themselves on the streets with mouths to feed, and for many, prostitution offers a quick fix. A local Pakistani prostitute can earn between 2,000 rupees (US$28) and 3,000 rupees (US$41) per day compared to the average monthly income of 2,500 rupees (US$35).

Forced prostitution is not rare. During hard times, women are often exploited and pushed into prostitution. Sandra (not her real name) said that after the death of her father she was left alone; friends and relatives deserted her after the grieving period. As a middle-class, educated woman she was surprised to find herself forced from her office job and into prostitution.

"My boss initially spoiled me at first," she told *Khaleej Times*. "[But] now I am in [the sex industry]." Sandra first thought her boss was being gracious, but quickly learned he was grooming her for sex for his own pleasure, and then acting as her pimp.

Many of Pakistan's contemporary sexual mores may have evolved from traditional practices. For example, polygamy, permitted in Muslim societies, stemmed from the need for larger family units which are better for supporting familial ties and tending for widows. Until such ancient customs are updated, women such as Sandra will continue to be bought and sold.

It's time for Pakistan to admit that prostitution is doing a roaring trade within its borders, and will continue to prosper until it is addressed in a modern manner. Let us hope that the people and government of this proud Muslim country will stop pretending the problem simply isn't there.

First published May 17, 2008 in *Asia Times Online*

Afterword

The research and reporting I have done over the years on sex in Asia has informed, educated, and sometimes startled me. I have found it personally fulfilling, and have attempted to share that with others through my writing.

Reflecting on the content that has made this book, I realized that very little emphasis was placed on a subject that I often dedicate time to: sexual health. Sexually transmitted diseases—from minor ones to the most feared HIV/AIDS—are very real challenges facing many societies throughout the world and the Asian community.

Great strides that were made, especially in Thailand for example, during the 1990s and early twenty-first century seem, at times, to be eroding. During that period there was much emphasis on education and prevention as these were at the forefront of sexual health. Yet in recent years a sort of complacency has set in and a lackadaisical approach has been taken by many, as if the problem has already been solved. I assure you, it has not.

We still need to protect ourselves and those we love using methods, particularly condoms, to ensure that we are around for the next party and romp. I know that at times I have represented this differently in my own experiences as described in this book, but I can assure you there is nothing enjoyable about sleepless nights and awaiting medical results. I have been lucky.

The women of Asia, or of anywhere in the world for that matter, whether bargirls or CEOs, deserve respect; whatever their position is in society, they have most often struggled to get there. Show people respect and you are guaranteed to have a much better experience in all your relationships.

True sexual fulfillment is a product of knowledge and communication, another reason I decry a lack of sexual education. The communication factor is a key element that must be explored with your partner. Asian women—and men—can be more demure and shy than their Western counterparts, but this does not mean that in a relationship a couple cannot find the same pleasures through trust and experimentation that other cultures enjoy.

I am reminded and entertained by a recent experience. As a sex columnist I occasionally receive sex toys from companies as samples in the hopes of a positive review. After I brought home a recent example of this bounty and was unpacking it, my wife responded with what amounted to: "What the hell is that?"

After explaining that it was a vibrating device meant for female stimulation, to enhance a couple's sex life, I was met with the equivalent retort of, "Well you can stick that up your *** but it is not coming anywhere near me." Nonetheless, she said this with a measure of good humor while playing with the buzzing vibe in her hands.

It was only through communication and trust in our relationship that some time later she agreed to experiment. Through a mix of oral stimulation augmented by the buzzing instrument, she found the effect joyously welcome, and has since accepted its occasional use in our interactions as a useful tool to enhance sexual pleasure.

Communication was the key, just as a moderately educated view on sexuality was in our relationship. Gently bring these elements into the relationships you have in Asia or beyond and the results will be tremendous.

Sex creates complex issues among humans, sometimes far

more than warranted. Remove man-made legislation, religious compunction, and ultra-moralist views and it becomes as natural as it is for any other creatures on the planet. Then remove pedophilia, sexual exploitation, and coercive sexual relationships, and we are left only with what is natural and appropriate.

In the foreword of this book, Simon Tearack refers to a goddess-like worship of nubile young women in the Asian sex trade that some Westerners can fall into. From another perspective, men should be careful not to become one of the hardcore "sexpats" of Asia. Often grizzled, cold, and devoid of emotion, these men can fall into the slavery of the sex industry that some believe is only the realm of the women who ply the trade.

While they may think of themselves as masters or aficionados of the sex trade, they are, in fact, usually expressing some downfall or failure that affected them at some time in their lives. Others may sit and listen to their stories in rapt attention, but unless they are also sexpats, they will usually walk away either wondering what would push a person to behave in such a way, or feeling a twinge of pity.

I once had an acquaintance who exceeded this sexpat stereotype. With stunning regularity, he woke early to exercise, have breakfast, work for a bit, and then head out for his midday sex romp at one of the innumerable daytime short-time establishments. Returning home to work for the afternoon, he would then head out again in the early evening to find another young woman to have sex with and return home to sleep—only to repeat this same exercise the next day.

One day, we stopped at a small grocery store on the way to his place. I watched as he got a bottle of milk and walked to the cash register, where he proceeded to empty an entire shelf of condoms into his shopping basket.

That certainly was amusing, and to those Westerners living a life with less sex than they would prefer, his lifestyle might seem like something to be envied. However, months later it became evident that he was depressed, unhappy, and living a life he found utterly unfulfilling. Even a living, breathing, beautiful female can become nothing more than a masturbation aid through over-indulgence.

The thrill of the chase, the moment when innocent romance turns sexual, the erotic delight of exploring your lover's body, the longing in absence that turns to lust upon her return, the communication between you and your partner about what makes you shudder in ecstasy—most, if not all, of these things are lost in the world of short-time sexual experiences with working girls.

Certainly handing a *mamasan* THB1,000 (US$30) for "Number 26" doesn't qualify as the chase, and the resulting encounter is likely to be about as romantic as any hour-long timed sexual interaction can be.

I am certainly not saying not to have fun, experiment, and indulge a bit—or maybe even a lot. From what I have written in this book you can see I too am not a saint by any stretch of the imagination. But in the same way that you should respect others no matter the circumstances, it is as important to remember to respect yourself too.

When the light fades and the daze subsides, we must all deal with the reality of our encounters.

Until next time, stay safe and have fun!

Acknowledgements

For my family: Mom, Denise, Luis, my wife Noi, and in memory of my father—this one is for you guys.

Thanks to my friends and editors David and Charles for their extracurricular work to support this effort.

To everyone at Monsoon Books, especially Phil and Natalie; thanks for taking a chance on me.

Asia Times Online and all the guys there, thanks for putting up with me—your advice, thoughts and ideas have been invaluable.

Finally, thanks to Marco, Robin, and Lee at *Asian Sirens* for the contributions you have made to my reporting and website over the years.